ZERI **Management Stories**

Out
OF THE
Box

*21 inspiring tales to create
and innovate at work*

by Gunter PAULI

ZERI - (Zero Emissions Research and Initiatives)

ZERI is a not-for-profit network of scholars and vigorous operators supported by scientists who wish to design and implement creative solutions to the pressing problems of our time. It is our desire to respond to the basic needs of people with what they have.

ISBN 1-920019-40-5

Published by Future Managers (Pty) Ltd
58 Polo Road, Observatory, 7925, South Africa

Printed and bound by Creda Communicactions

For inquiries on ZERI in your language, email one of the following:

Spanish
Dr. Carlos Bernal
Director del Instituto ZERI para Latino America, Bogota, Colombia
bernal@zeri.org

English
Dr. Mike Agho
Director of the ZERI Center in Bauchi, Nigeria
info@zeri.org

Ms. Nirmala Nair
Director, ZERI-Southern Africa
Cape Town, South Africa
nair@zeri.org

Mrs. Lynda Taylor and *Robert Haspel*
Co-directors of SCI/ZERI New Mexico, Santa Fe, NM, USA
taylor@zeri.org or haspel@zeri.org

Portuguese
Prof. Lucio Brusch, Chairman of ZERI Brasil, Curitiba, Brazil
lucio@zeri.org

Japanese
Mrs. Miyako Yoshino, Representative Director of ZERI Education Japan,
Kamakura, Japan
yoshino@zeri.org

German
Mrs. Tina Schmidt, President ZERI Germany, Berlin, Germany
tina@zeri.org

TABLE OF CONTENTS

A Word of Thanks

After having published 12 books in 12 languages, my two young sons, Carl-Olaf and Laurenz-Frederik were the ones who inspired me to write fairy tales. How else could I explain to them why I am so often absent, other than in writing? A father belongs with his family. But with this calling to change the world for the better, searching to translate scientific findings into concrete projects, believing that one can make a major difference in the world, the attraction remained too strong.

Although I have a sense of failure as a dad, I wished to contribute something unique and special: fairy tales written for them, explaining the core of my work, bringing insights to the centre of my passion. The first fable was written in 1997: "How Can I Be The Strongest Tree?" It was in response to the misleading phrase "survival of the fittest", which justifies aggression, cheating and fear since "not everyone will make it". The concept of the survival of the fittest justifies harm to others and only the strongest survive? My work brings a different message.

While working in Colombia, it struck me that the Latin Americans are prepared to farm French mushrooms (Champignons de Paris) in the tropics, but no Frenchmen would consider farming coffee in Paris. This led to my second fable, "Growing Coffee in Paris" - the children loved it and wanted more. Soon there was a story on the double moral in our society "Can I Steal Less?" And we all know how we have to remind our children to brush their teeth, which led to yet another tale: "Why can't I eat sugar?"

By the turn of the century I had a dozen stories written. The publication of the "Tree Story" at the World Expo in Germany led to an immediate and spontaneous translation into over 100 languages. Twenty-seven versions were printed and over 1 million copies distributed. The illustrations by Pamela Salazar Ocampo quickly became a global success. Yet this was only the beginning. The City of Curitiba decided to expose all their school children to the fairy tales. Some 120,000 small, folded booklets were made available to kids, for free, bringing the zest of science to them in a playful, easy-to-understand format. I turned out to be an inspiring dad for many kids around the world. That was a surprise.

When management (who are also mums and dads), experienced these tales, they were met with great enthusiasm. Corporations ranging from HSBC in London, Petrobras in Brazil, Taiheyo Cement in Japan, Unilever in the Netherlands and Bavaria in Colombia requested concrete examples that would clarify the cases, and on the basis of my 30 years of experience with business, these cases were provided quickly. Ideas began to develop on how business could become more creative, innovative and demonstrate leadership. The way to get management to think out of the box happened to be the same fairy tales that inspired my two boys. And so this book was born!

I am indebted to Suzanne Fielden, who has accompanied my work for the ZERI Foundation since 1995, for encouraging me to take the time to compile the stories from the management angle; to Pamela Salazar Ocampo for the magnificent illustrations; to Carlos Bernal for securing the first edition in the Spanish version for Colombia; to Tina Schmidt for pushing me to make this book a priority at a time when I had four other manuscripts to deal with; to JaDe Forster for giving the editing a first crack and Nirmala Nair who not only gave the editing a second crack but also ensured that the book got published in the wonderful biosphere of Cape Town, South Africa, for the world to read, and, of course, I owe it to my boys for making it all happen with so much joy. I am proud of them, and hope they will be proud of me one day!

A big thank you to Yazeed Fakir for generously giving his time to tidy up and do the last minute proof reading...

Gunter Pauli
Kamakura, Japan, 31st of July 2004

INTRODUCTION

Management with Leadership will always improve the performance of a company. We are living in a world characterized by over-supply where customers choose and competition thrives. Business must improve its performance beyond satisfying shareholders and stakeholders. It must respond to the needs of the consumer.

But an entirely new bottom line is emerging. There are millions who lack water, food, health-care, decent housing and education. There are at least one billion without jobs and the numbers are rising. The needs are tremendous, yet we face a world characterized by scarcity, operating in a market characterized by over-supply. So what is missing to develop this huge market driven by demand for a just and joyful world without hunger or poverty?

The present economic system is claimed to be the 'best' we've ever had in history, but it certainly has a lot of room for improvement and progress. Indeed, our business and social system is currently showing critical signs of weakness and the next decade will weed out those who do not re-invent their business strategies and true leadership etiquette. At the same time, those who do re-invent will not only be significantly more profitable, but will place business firmly at the center of society, responding to societies' desires and needs – beyond those of the shareholders.

Business today is driven by MBAs and cash flow analysts trained at the best schools around the world – and yet they work at barely 10% resource efficiency. Imagine if only 10% of your workforce actually worked? According to current statistics, we waste 90% of our resources! Imagine what we can do if we achieved 100% resource efficiency and added value to our products and services all the time. The world would be a very different place. And the global economy would be one of abundance, and not the current model of scarcity.

Our current business system must, therefore, have pioneering leaders who are prepared to acknowledge that *it is up for a major improvement and overhaul,* and to have the creativity, courage and innovation to change the way things are done – through an insatiable quest for knowledge that goes way beyond the curriculum of schools and universities! This dynamism would permeate the entire work place – elevating all those within it and creating better results for the customer, shareholder and the Earth's resources, through such intelligent and long over-due leadership.

In reality, this is not a matter of choice - it is a matter of survival.

If management aims only at being as good as it was before, it will simply maintain its present position. Mature products and business models demand a continuous quest for innovation, a willingness to embrace discontinuity instead of being stuck in continuity (predictability). Those businesses which cling to previous successes without a permanent drive towards innovation, will lose market share and suffer from less customer loyalty, which ultimately – but quickly – translates into lower margins, and stressful announcements of lowering profits, missed sales targets, downsizing and lay-offs.

We also have to remember that we are dealing with increasing consumer awareness as we surf through the information age. Long-term success depends on an organization's capacity to anticipate change and subsequent market trends. Better still, instead of undergoing changes, and running after them, smart corporations create shifts in the market they want, whenever and wherever they see a gap emerging. Such leadership requires creativity and innovation at all levels, while remaining in touch with the real needs and desires of the people; and the limitations imposed by the immediate environment in which they operate. It requires the capacity to take risks.

Today, meeting sales targets, increasing market share and improving return on capital is the absolute *minimum* requirement. It seems that the only effective strategy to achieve this is through mergers with competitors, downsizing middle management, enforcing a standardized supply chain management and outsourcing production. But has this really brought the best to market? Slashing expenses and taking control of competitors may have been the option in the 1980s and 1990s - but it certainly did not bring more innovation and leadership to business, only "power" measured in terms of market capitalization and chief executive bonus systems.

The time has come to bring PASSION back into business. And this goes beyond making the company fun to work for. Consider pioneering a system which makes real sense by adding value to all global and local stakeholders. I challenge you to BECOME part of a SYSTEM where everyone is winning except your competitors, who are still doing things the "old way". They simply do not have the right to remain in the market and the conscious consumer will boot them out. Marketing prescribes that we should only make what people really want, not what we entice them to buy. With the weakening of purchasing power, time has come for businesses to go beyond the obvious, and search for what will become very obvious in years to come. The time has come to get out of the box, that black box - of tried and tested formulas.

Creativity and innovation are the engines of the economy, it is the basis of competitiveness, hence the need to invest in research and development. Whilst governments and large corporations invest zillions of dollars, small entrepreneurs bring innumerable inventions to market without subsidies or tax breaks. They see the potential and launch their innovation, often changing a paradigm forever. Often they are bought out by the "fat cats" and their innovation is shelved in order to avoid their outdated product from becoming obsolete. This is to escape the expenses incurred through the necessary updating of production equipment... as in the typical case of Monsanto, which bought out the patents of Biopol, a plastic made by bacteria.

After decades of talk about entrepreneurship, I asked myself what was the best tool to unleash creativity and innovation, so that it could permeate all the work we do, wherever we are in the world and wherever we'd like to operate. In this book, my goal is to unleash your creativity and innovation – cutting you loose to change the way you do business, forever. And the way to get the process going is through fairy tales. It is archaic to believe that in order to succeed in business (eating an egg) you have to create some damage elsewhere (breaking the egg). In order for someone to win, someone else has to lose: that is the old business logic. Here is a new one.

In order to unleash your creativity, innovation and leadership, we opted for a strategy that has been proven for centuries: *fables, fairy tales and stories...* Wisdom has been passed on from culture to culture, from generation to generation all over the world through imaginary stories, which speak to our imagination, which tantalize our creativity and which call upon our leadership to pursue what seems like a dream. The stories in the book seem like a dream when we are children, but they actually become reality when we are ready.

These fables and fairy tales are written with the same spirit and wit that drove the famous Jean de la Fontaine, Hans Christian Andersen and the Brothers Grimm. But there is one major difference: every fairy tale is based on science, and even though at first it seems unreal, the clever reality of science and the market soon becomes obvious. These stories inspire management to be creative, innovative – and fantastic, creating the same feeling a child has after listening to a bedtime story. The difference is, a child goes to sleep and sleeps well after hearing the same story for the tenth time; when management hears these stories - they won't be able to go to bed!

The stories in this book explain how creativity, innovation and leadership can be implemented at work and subsequently translated into the world. It's about *teamwork, going against the tide, doubling productivity, finding revenues where no one else has ventured, looking for hidden assets and treasures, identifying new sources of energy, maintaining high ethical standards, attracting cohesive talent, inspiring future generations* - and so much more. These tales are easy to understand and quick to put into practice. It will soon be clear that creativity, innovation and leadership are not mutually exclusive with hard bottom line results; on the contrary these are pre-conditions. The crux is that even an eggshell can be of great use after scrambled eggs! Did you know that it is rich in calcium and that once you remove the membrane you can generate electricity with it, provided you have some potassium?

These tales have inspired millions of children around the world. It helps them to boost their academic learning, strengthens their emotional intelligence, and builds their capacity to express themselves through art and to become great *system thinkers* – something our education has fallen far short of equipping us for. Yet we cannot blame anyone; the world is changing faster than we ever imagined.

Complex and chaotic situations are not difficult to grasp, discontinuity will become the norm, as well as responding to the needs of people, societies and the environment. Children today will be the leaders of the future. We urge current executives to wake up that child in you, whatever your age, to rekindle that open minded, eager, enthused adventurer who is ready to shape the world intelligently, whilst having fun in the process. This new corporate leader and his team will see and understand the many transformations in the economy both now and for future generations. We are on the brink of working together, to reach common goals, which are now becoming an essential part of our reality.

The tales in this book have been tested in many languages and exposed to managers in dozens of countries, including Japan, Sweden, Italy, France, Spain, UK, Germany, Brazil and USA and in developing nations such as Ecuador, Colombia, Zimbabwe, Namibia, Nigeria, Indonesia, India and China. The response to these fairy tales was so enthusiastic that I decided to bring these together into one simple book: **Out of The Box**. Our creativity is boxed in by the linear business paradigm and the time has come to break the box and unleash the creativity and innovative spirit.

Remember the Egg of Columbus, the navigator who discovered America? He asked how one could make an egg stand up. After numerous trials everyone gave up. Then he simply took a hard boiled egg, crushed its bottom and placed it on the table. The question was simple and the answer was evident as long as one was prepared to think out of the box. Remember the exercise of the nine dots which you have to connect with four straight lines without lifting the pen from the paper? Today there are even multiple solutions which only require one line! Can you imagine getting so far out of the box? That is what is urgently needed for business today.

The following 21 fairy tales prepare companies, executives and their teams to be the pioneering agents of transformation, as well as promising to be both fun and profitable. Each concept is clarified with a concrete, brief business case. Some are successes, some failures. Examples are based on first-hand experiences from 20 different companies, some large multinationals, some small niche players, some venture capital-funded innovation companies operating in Europe, North and South America, Asia and Africa. Creativity and innovation are not the exclusive domain of the North and the multinational corporation; it also is happening in the Southern Hemisphere. Those executives who embrace these concepts of creativity, innovation and leadership will bring business to the forefront of society, responding to people's requirements in co-evolution with nature, strengthening culture and tradition, as well as creating a wonderful platform upon which entrepreneurs will thrive, wherever they are in the world...

Through the writing of this book, if I am given an opportunity to contribute towards a new wave of entrepreneurship, creativity, innovation and leadership around the world, then I will have achieved more than I could have dreamed when writing these stories for my two sons, Carl-Olaf and Laurenz-Frederik, supporting their innocence and faith - that this world is a great place in which to grow up and live ...

What is ZERI?

ZERI is the acronym for Zero Emissions Research and Initiatives. It started in 1991 when I imagined a production system without any form of "waste". The first article on this concept was published in Korea. The world of ideas has gone global indeed. It seemed impossible until 1994 when I was given the opportunity to create a network of scientists who would jointly search for creative solutions to the world's most pressing problems.

With the support of Prof. Dr. Heitor Gurgulino de Souza, Rector of the United Nations University, and Prof. Dr. Carl-Göran Hedén, MD, member of the Royal Swedish Academy of Sciences, a platform of creativity and innovation was converted to a series of projects which demonstrated through trial and error that these fantastic ideas were not only scientifically correct, but also made business sense.

Thanks to these efforts there are now dozens of projects being created, implemented in schools and universities on four continents, while simultaneously entrepreneurs and management wonder how they can dramatically increase productivity, create more jobs and have a sense of fulfilment in their work.

Today, ZERI is an international network of project offices, NGOs and foundations, which focus on:
- Design and implementation of projects;
- Exposing the youth in our communities to these opportunities through education;
- Enabling everyone to make a positive difference, including business; and,
- Assistance in terms of both vision and the tools.

The youngest addition to the network is ZERI Southern Africa. Thanks to the unrelenting drive and the positive energy of Nirmala Nair, who spared no effort to prepare herself for the challenge, the network is expanding in Africa. She has a clear commitment to make a difference for the people who we seldom have a chance to reach out to: the farmers, the fishermen, single mothers and children. The remarkable challenge she accepted is to demonstrate that a new type of development is possible: one that makes a difference on the ground, while contributing to a new model for development that thrives on the exceptional natural resources Southern Africa is entrusted with, and the wealth of cultural diversity that characterizes this promising part of the world, provided its citizens realize what they have.

For further information visit **www.zeri.org.**

Chapter 1
Redefining Competitiveness

How a new vision is reshaping competitive forces

If we maintain the present,
we are certain to lose a better future.
To seize that better future,
we must go beyond what is considered best today.

When we study biology at high school, we are taught to classify life into the plant and animal kingdoms. Some even think that mankind belongs to a separate kingdom. All too often we are not aware there are Five Kingdoms of Nature: animals, plants, fungi, algae (protoctista) and bacteria (monera).

When we study chemistry at high school, we are taught to divide everything into the the organic and inorganic. We forget that each kingdom of nature has such a distinct organic and inorganic chemistry.

When we study physics at high school, we are taught how an apple falls to Earth. No one bothered to explain how the components of the apple got up there in the first place, bluntly defying the law of gravity.

When we study engineering at high school, we are taught how to put things together faster and better. No engineer learns with the same zeal how to take things apart.

When we study mathematics at high school, we are taught how to configure linear mathematical models. But in nature, just about everything follows non-linear paths and we have to wait until we are undertaking post-graduate studies before this comes to order.

When we study business at high school, we are taught to focus on cashflow and the core business. Business – through market forces- is supposed to allocate scarce resources to the most efficient operators. But while millions live in poverty, markets are characterized by over-supply, and waste accumulates everywhere. No business can remain disconnected from life on Earth.

When we study ethics in school, we are taught not to steal. Stealing less is not good enough. But then we offer national awards for companies for polluting less. Yet these corporations continue to pollute! Can you be released from jail for promising to steal less? How come you become a hero for polluting less?

If we want business to be competitive, we have to go beyond the present concept of strengths and weaknesses, opportunities and threats. If we want business to be competitive and sustainable, the present tools do not satisfy at all. So let us go on a path that has influenced business and society at large many times before: creativity, innovations and leadership.

If we want our children to live in a sustainable world, then the time has come to go beyond the concept of sustainability that was adopted 20 years ago. While organic food was a logical response to the excessive use of harmful pesticides in the Sixties, the mere elimination of these pesticides does not really make the produce sustainable. Certified organic food indicates what it does not contain, though what we need to know is what it does, and where it comes from. How else will business be able to provide depth to the product and gain the customer loyalty it seeks.

Consider the following definition of competitiveness: "The capacity to respond to consumer needs, with increasingly less resources, generating ever more value for all stakeholders involved." Now consider a new definition for sustainability: "The capacity to respond to the basic needs of all species, in co-evolution with each other." The basic human needs are water, food, shelter, energy, health, learning and jobs. The time has come to recognize that the way the world works, and the way we should design products, manufacturing and consumption, is fundamentally different today - and requires different basic skills than those we were taught at our best business schools a few decades ago.

Unless we unlearn the current vision of reality and the way business competes (which changes all the time), it will be impossible for our children or grandchildren to ever live in a world characterized by abundance, where all basic needs are met, especially of the poor and the marginalized. Corporations that seize the opportunity will be the winners of the future.

CHAPTER 2
THE FIVE KINGDOMS OF NATURE AND THE FOUR DESIGN PRINCIPLES

THE 1ST DESIGN PRINCIPLE

No one species eats its own waste; whatever is waste for one, is food for another species belonging to another kingdom.

If one species starts to eat its own waste it will deteriorate. When cattle farmers started to feed cows with waste from other cows they violated this principle - and it led to the outbreak of mad cow disease. Shrimp farmers made the same mistake when shrimps were fed their own waste - leading to white shrimp virus.

A lion will eat an antelope, but would a lion consider the manure of the antelope? There are exceptions which confirm the rule; ocasionally a dog may be spotted eating its own waste, though this is a matter of strengthening, challenging its immune system. If an animal were only ingesting its own waste, and behave as a cannibal, it would never survive.

If industry were to re-use all its own waste, then it decreases its flexibility and increases the risk of failure.

The waste of one industry should be used as a value-added input for another industry.

If one species is fed its own waste, it will degenerate.

THE 2ND DESIGN PRINCIPLE

Whatever is a toxin for a species belonging to one kingdom will be neutral, or a nutrient, for another species in at least one other kingdom.

As humans we tend to classify things that are toxic only from a human point of view. We assume that anything that is toxic for us must also be toxic for all other species in every kingdom. In addition, we view viruses as universally dangerous. The reality, though, is that viruses are kingdom-specific and can be eliminated if we apply the first design principle.

The reason why the slaughter-house practice of boiling waste meat prior to feeding it to other cattle won't necessarily work is precisely because of the first design principle. The prion causing madcow disease could survive high temperatures. To eliminate the prion or a virus, the left-over waste meat must go through the other 4 kingdoms. Cyanide and Arseincum are well known toxin for animals, but several plant species produce it and use it effectively as a defense against predators. Apples are rich in cyanide, and so are peaches, though none of these have to be labeled "dangerous – cyanide inside".

If you have a problem with an old gold mine, and cyanide leaching, simply plant an apple orchard and over the years the toxins will be eliminated. Probably, the cyanide will be gone well before the lawyers will come to a final agreement settling on responsibilities and costs.

If one species eliminates toxins or viruses within its own system, it will degenerate.

The 3rd design principle

The more diverse and local the systems, the more efficient and resilient their operations. When systems are more efficient and more resilient, the more diverse and the more local they are operating.

A group of plants and trees in a temperate climate do not feel the need to bring some fungi from the tropics. The plants and trees in co-existence and in co-evolution with species belonging to the other four kingdoms will create the best, most effective system from within the boundaries of its own micro system.

Relating this to our global economy we see that we want everything from everywhere at any place and time. We have increased the fragility of our own system because if one or two links break, the whole system could fall apart. The more local the activities, the stronger they are – and there will be much more flexibility as diversity increases. A system that is local will be more efficient and resilient.

Companies are in search of local supply and better integration into the local economy. Whereas global (out)sourcing, supply chain management and customer relations are considered key components of a successful business, the capacity to be local globally requires a new wave of creative and innovative strategies.

If non-native species are forced to become part of the ecosystem, it will degenerate.

THE 4TH DESIGN PRINCIPLE

All kingdoms combined, integrate and separate matter at ambient temperature and pressure.

A spider makes its nylon-like fiber at ambient temperature and pressure, from diverse raw materials. The moment the tension drops, it starts disintegrating. The spider operates at ambient temperature and pressure with fungi in its guts, and bacteria to control the process, with plant components as food. The mollusk in the cold water produces a ceramic that is stronger than bullet-proof ceramic. In nature, no one knows how to make fire or change pressure at will, yet products from nature outperform human made artefacts.

Industry has set up a supply chain management which delivers components within very precise and uniform parameters. All assembly and disassembly requires high temperature and pressure, causing pollution and entropy. It is considered that the use of chemistry, temperature and pressure speed up production and facilitates standardization. Creativity and innovation on the other hand is the only way to find the best of both worlds.

If industry emulates the "all-inclusive approach" of nature, it will be able to produce more efficiently, at lower, cost-slashing energy needs. Whereas this seems impossible today, it is this type of creative approach that requires a passion for thinking out of the box. This requires taking risks. This is the unique role corporations must assume.

When matter is integrated and separated beyond the energy provided by the sun, without taking into consideration the specific involvement of each of the five kingdoms, the process will cause entropy.

When business understands the five kingdoms and the four design principles, as well as the principle of sustainability as defined before, then it will realize that there is a tremendous potential for creativity, innovation and leadership redefining the competitive framework of business for decades to come.

"Go beyond the obvious!"

Can Apples Fly?

An owl sits on the branch of an apple tree laden with apples that are ready to drop.

"Did you know people can calculate how fast an apple falls to the ground?" says the owl to a mouse enjoying some food.

"I am not interested in that, I am hungry," says the mouse.

"You <u>should</u> be interested. This is science, and you would learn a lot from what people find out about how nature really works…"

"People have no idea how nature works," snaps the mouse.

"You arrogant little rat! Do you know more than the people who call themselves Homo sapiens?"

"I do not know more, but at least I do not pretend that I can explain everything with some magic called mathematics."

"But these formulas are not magic, they allow us to understand, to be precise, to be exact."

"Do you have a feather?" asks the mouse of the owl.

"Sure, I am a bird."

"Then drop one," suggests the mouse.

The owl pulls out a feather with his beak, and drops it. The wind carries it around and floats it through the air, and about one minute later, nearly out of sight, it lands on the ground.

"So, wise owl, what's the formula for your Homo sapiens now?"

"It does not work, but that is because of the wind and the pressure."

"So why don't you add that to the formula?" says the mouse.

"I can't figure it out; do you know the trick?"

"I have no idea. People do not know either; they should be called Homo *no* sapiens."

"That's not a very nice thing to say!"

"Can apples fly?"

"Stop joking. You know apples do not have wings. Birds have wings".

"Well, I am tired of hearing about apples falling to the ground. What I want to know is how the apple got up there in the first place!"

© 1997 Pauli

An Inspiration for Management:
GO BEYOND THE OBVIOUS

If you want to innovate, you have to go beyond the obvious. The insight on how to design a new product, or a new system for a client, depends on your team's capacity to search for insights and explanations which are self-evident, yet no one else has thought of. **Explain the obvious,** especially if this has not been explained to you before.

An abundance of wisdom means nothing if everyone knows it, can learn it and can apply it - like learning a mathematical formula by heart. The obvious must be explained in layman's terms. Complex concepts and scientific jargon will not get the potentially innovative alternatives understood by management, and would certainly not reach the board of directors who usually have little time for change. Whatever is **complex should be rephrased in the form of an easy question.**

If no one has been able to explain this new idea in simple terms, then you must be open to alternatives, which may include conflicting insights. Do not expect innovative ideas to be expressed in a precise mathematical formula or business plan. Innovative ideas require creative, imaginative and artistic forms of expression, some symbolism and a clear-cut case so that the vision emerges. **The right questions will formulate a new vision.** That is the basis for entrepreneurship.

BULMERS CIDER VS BACARDI BREEZER

When the leading British leading cider-maker Bulmers, a US$700 million market leader and the producer of brands like Strong Bow, felt massive competition from the new popular alcoholic drinks like Bacardi Breezer or Smirnoff Ice, it sought to reposition itself in the market in the niche that had recently been created. This was the obvious strategy.

The problem was that as a niche player, with cider playing only a minor role in the overall alcoholic beverage market, going against strong marketing brands like Bacardi and Smirnoff was not an easy one. The reaction of the CEO, Mike Hughes, a former top executive in the Guinness beer group, was to build a global brand. A brand that one day could compete with the Bacardi and Smirnoff successes. This would only be possible if there were years of vast advertising budgets available. This was the obvious strategy, but cash simply was not available.

The US marketing team could very well get nationwide distribution as part of that strategy to position a global brand, but could only get Strong Bow on the shelves, it just could not move the product. Market demand was either for the Breezers or Ices. The management insisted on an advertising drive to sell the chosen brand, Strong Bow, but the actual bestseller in the portfolio of Bulmer's was Woodchuck, and it remained in that top spot without any marketing support or push.

Why was Woodchuck so successful? When one considers the "Vermontness" of this product, one begins to understand the attraction to the market. A company like Horizon (producer of organic milk) paid millions of dollars in order to get access to the "Milk from Vermont" branding. So when Bulmers was looking for a solution to its new competitive framework, it stayed with the same logic that its CEO knew when he was the President of Guinness USA: get the nationwide distribution, push your one strong brand globally, especially in the USA. In the meantime, the market was buying a premium product which was not promoted at all.

When one realizes that the USA facility was only operating at 20% capacity, this local product could be successfully promoted. Since this Woodchuck did not need specially-produced apples, it could take the left-overs from organic apple farms and convert their low quality apples with no market value in a prime cider that the market would cherish since it was made in...Vermont. Bulmers did not follow this advice. The CEO made an additional advertising push, which failed. He had to resign. Soon after, Bulmers was acquired for a small price by Newcastle and the family lost control of a business it had been growing for 4 generations.

Whereas everyone is looking at how to position a brand with heavy advertising spending, let us not forget how many brands started in the first place: small. The growing of a brand over time, in line with the possibilities of the cash flow that is generated, is more important than the quick harvesting of a fruit. Every apple defies the law of gravity before actually submitting itself to it.

Explain the obvious by asking simple questions about complex issues
This helps to create a vision and new insights which is the basis of entrepreneurship

Let's figure out how the apple got up there

"Going against the Flow"

Are Butterflies Drunk?

A trout seems motionless as he faces upstream in a small river, and he sees a butterfly in the air.

"Are you drunk?" bubbles the trout, "why can't you fly straight?"

"I just follow the energy," laughs the butterfly.

"What do you mean? There is no energy in the air, energy comes from the sun."

"No, energy from the sun is mainly for plants. We butterflies get our energy from very tiny whispers of wind…"

"So you are windsurfing?" wondered the trout.

"Exactly! We fly wherever the little wind takes us, but since there is so much here and there, we get bounced around anywhere and everywhere!"

"Now I understand. You are not drunk, you just hang in the wind and go with the flow. That's smart," replied the trout.

"I know you can't possibly be drunk," mused the butterfly. "But how do you manage to swim so still in this big rush of water?"

"It's easy. I use the power of the water rushing downwards."

"You must be joking. I would have thought the water would push you down the river!"

"No, rushing water gives me the strength to jump forward, unless there's danger – I'm able to literally shoot forward."

"Impossible," says the butterfly, "I just saw a young man wading in the water; he could not even walk where you are now appearing perfectly still!"

"That is because he is not made for walking in the water, he is made for walking on land."

"You mean water flowing downwards gives you the strength to swim upwards?"

"Exactly, whenever there is a force that goes down, there is a force that to goes up too."

"But how can water rush down, while it makes you rush up?"

"Look at me, I have the shape of an egg."

"You, shaped like an egg? From up here you look more like half a boomerang."

"Silly you. Thanks to my egg-shaped head, water flows into my face, it whirls around and then turns in the other direction. The harder it flows down, the stronger it can push me up!"

"Wonderful. So you look like an egg, while swimming effortlessly against the flow of a river, and I look like a drunk, surfing in quiet air... but we both use the energy to go wherever we want to go and people have no clue how we do it!"

© 2001 Pauli

An Inspiration for Management:
GOING AGAINST THE FLOW

If you do what everyone else does, you will end up having low margins. If you wish to have higher margins, you cannot simply imitate others. Innovation requires you to go against the flow, creating a new stream of revenue, which others will have to follow as you take market share. **Do not do what others do.** The butterfly and the trout get energy from sources we never imagined were of use.

If you understand how others achieve their objectives, then you will become more aware of how you can be innovative, by doing something unique without others necessarily understanding how you did it! This broader understanding of how someone who is not a competitor can get to where he wants to very efficiently, gives you the strength to **pursue a unique and surprising avenue that others do not understand.**

The power of having a unique selling proposition is that you do not patent your technology; this way you do not divulge your technique. You simply mass-produce without giving explanations. The longer others do not understand how you are succeeding, the better your position in the market place. Do what you do best, **which is finding unique angles,** especially when no one has a clue. That is the basis for securing your position.

ECOVER GOES TO THE SUPERMARKETS

When the environmental detergent company Ecover decided to distribute through supermarkets, its competitors from the environmental manufacturers decided that this was equivalent to treason. The health food market threatened to discontinue selling the washing products the day Ecover hit the shelves. The risk was great that entering the large retail chains would undermine the loyalty of the health food stores, which had been loyal to real ecological products. The opportunity to have an environmental product on the shelves of a Sainsbury in the UK or an ICA in Sweden back in the 1990s was unique. Indeed, the large retailers would not allow two or three outspoken green products on their shelves. When one realizes that there is only space for ONE, and this one could be you, you have to go against the current and leap forward.

The risk was considered great that the health food trade would side with a smaller green producer but one that had a pronounced environmental profile. Since there were enough competitors that would have been glad to take Ecover's space in the health food stores, something unique was needed to mitigate the risk. In order to overcome this risk, a grand strategy was designed which included the construction of an ecological factory. This wooden factory, with a large grass roof, became a symbol of green entrepreneurship. It demonstrated that production could be as ecological as the formulation of the product itself.

This widely-publicized opening of an ecological factory made it impossible for the health food stores to give up this high-profile brand, which pushed the limits of ecology, from product formulation to production systems and factory design. The media attention made it difficult for the supermarkets not to carry the product either. The pressure on the supermarkets was so great that they even invited Ecover to place products on their shelves without the traditional slotting fees. They would also purchase direct without any intermediaries, offering increased margins that were never feasible through specialized distribution channels.

The green competitors and small manufacturers did not understand that the margins could be better with supermarkets than with health food stores. They believed that it was expensive to enter the supermarket; they had to pay for shelfspace, invest minimum spending for advertising and that regular promotions would dramatically decrease margins, plus that there would be a lot of pressure on the sales price. This would lead to a price difference with the health food store so that in the end this distribution channel would evaporate. As president of Ecover, I did not wish to clarify that the margins in the supermarkets were actually double the margins in the health food trade. And since we did not undertake any expensive advertising campaigns, we achieved a level of profitability which was incomparable with multinationals which spent heavily on promotions, and incomparable with the other green producers who could never get the high margins.

Don't do what others do
Pursue what others do not understand
Do what you do best, which equals no stress

Let us become windsurfers and learn to swim
effortlessly upstream, where others do not venture

"Problems are Opportunities"

The Five Kingdoms Of Nature

When the Earth was born... first life emerged in the form of the smallest, and even the invisible: bacteria.

Bacteria lived alone for a billion years. And since the Earth was then covered with water, they thrived in water.

In order to create more bacteria, they split into two and life started anew.

Some bacteria produced a lot of waste, in the form of oxygen. Slowly the air became filled with it. But there was too much and it was toxic.

Some bacteria learned how to breathe, to convert oxygen into energy and a new family was born...

The first kingdom of life, bacteria, now had two families: those who live without oxygen and those who live off oxygen.

Bacteria grew, friends and visitors, and even enemies shaped new forms of life by sticking together. When thousands of cells formed a new structure, a new type of life was born: the Protoctista. They look like algae, slime moulds. The Spirulina became the Queen of Protoctista...

And so a second kingdom emerged on Earth, and bacteria and algae lived happily together.

But something miraculous happened for the first time. The living creatures of the new Kingdom of Protoctista no longer just split into two; they actually reproduced when a male and a female were together!

A million years later, fungi and plants began to find their way into the world - first in water and later on land...

Plants and trees grew in harmony; fungi converted the waste from plants together with bacteria, and into food for the trees. Two more Kingdoms had emerged: the Kingdom of Plants, and the Kingdom of Fungi.

The Oak tree became the King of Plants; the Reishi became the King of Fungi. And all four of them lived happily together.

Cells began to take shape, producing limbs that enabled some to either run, fly or creep. Insects, fish, birds and mammals enriched life on Earth with the beautiful and diverse Kingdom of Animals. And the Lion became the King ...

And they lived happily together. Animals eat grass and plants, some like meat, and the "waste" is converted into humus... fungi produces nutrients and the only ones you cannot see are the bacteria, but they are everywhere!

After billions of years, one species - human beings - learned how to make fire whenever they wanted.

Today, it is still the only species that knows how to make fire - and many have had sleepless nights ever since.

© 2001 Pauli

Inspiration for Management:
PROBLEMS ARE OPPORTUNITIES

Ever since Peter Drucker stated the fact that *'Problems are Opportunities'*, management has tried to take a fresh look at problem-solving. Even a major problem millennia ago - oxygen - in fact led to a great innovation, which resulted in the birth of a new family of bacteria, and ultimately to mammals, including us, the human species. **Often the very moment of the deepest crisis is the basis for the greatest innovation.**

This implies that you cannot only work using the same familiar tools, and the same methods that have always helped to solve previous challenges. On the contrary, **whatever helped you solve the problems in the past; may very well be part of the problem today.**

Therefore, it is important to rely on a wide variety of options, and to explore choices, which are embedded in your markets. You just have to find them. The greater the diversity, the more likely and faster new solutions will emerge. **Challenges in a diverse environment have more opportunities.**

TAIHEYO CEMENT

The Japanese market for cement has been faced with a decreasing demand for its core product for over a decade. After years of unstoppable boom and expansion in construction, the bubble burst and demand collapsed. The market contracted and the industry suffered from major over-capacity. A merger of companies imposed itself; Taiheyo is the result of the combination of Nippon Cement, Chichibo Cement and Onoda Cement. Whereas the merger was logical, the closure of several plants was not, especially in the Japanese context of life-time employment. In addition, many facilities were considered "brown fields" and if the ongoing business was to be stopped, then a major clean-up cost would have had to be borne. So, when closing more plants does not make sense, another strategy imposes itself. A problem has to become an opportunity.

The key is to convert existing under-utilized and unprofitable businesses into a new business model which permits long-term viability. Taiheyo had attempted to offer "waste incineration", including toxic waste as a solution for its business but opposition from the public at large and the increased amount of residual toxic dust made Taiheyo decided that it did not want to pursue the route of incinerating industrial waste. But a new opportunity emerged. The City of Hidaka, situated in the vicinity of the Taiheyo plant in Saitama, was faced with a major challenge. The local landfill was filling up and no permission from the citizens to renew the incinerator was forthcoming.

Thanks to an American technology, reinforced with Swedish inventions, the defunct cement kilns could be converted to waste processing plants. The municipal solid waste, which had a high content of compostable material, was converted to a clean fuel through a combined aerobic and anaerobic process. In this way, the cement company could substitute one ton of imported coal with two tons of processed waste, from which all the toxic components which would have caused problems with air or soil contamination have been removed. Cement kilns are not used to simply burn, but to process waste in such a way that it generates a long-term business for a dysfunctional kiln, while relieving the city of the pressure and the cost to incinerate waste. It reduces imports of coal and substitutes these with a local product of which supply is guaranteed for decades to come. This reduces carbon emissions and contributes to the stabilization of the climate.

Deep crisis leads to innovation
Solutions of the past are often part of the problems of today
The more diverse the environment, the more solutions available.

We don't need any more animals making fire!

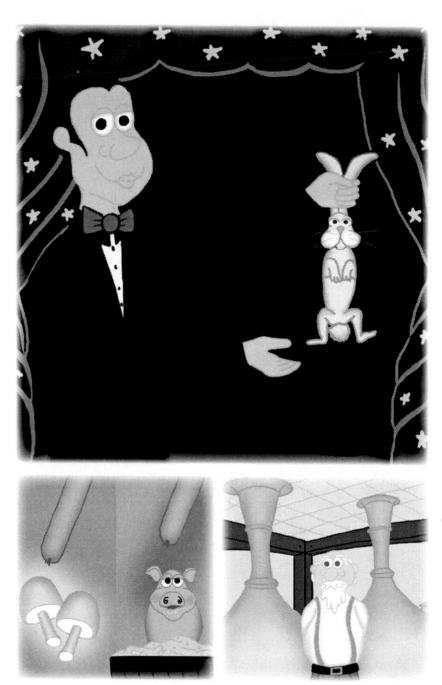

The Magic Hat

Robert is a magician. He is a sorcerer and makes things happen which no one else could ever have thought of. He is asked to visit and show his tricks to a beer brewer in Germany...

"Show me, what magic can you make happen in my little brewery?" asks the master brewer who makes the best lager.

"Hmmm, there seems to be so much in the air, but I cannot make it happen. Something is in the way!" says Robert.

"Tell me what is in the way, so that I can surprise all the children in town."

"I need some of your spent grain."

"Spent grain? You mean this trashy waste that I give to the cattle for feed?"

"Yes, give me the spent grain and I'll come back tomorrow."

The next day, the sorcerer returned with a loaf of bread.

"Oh, but that is not magic," responded the beer brewer, "We've made bread before - but now people want nice, soft, fresh bread with a crust on the outside."

"Over-fresh, but deep frozen with enzymes to make it crusty," responds the sorcerer. "That is easy to do. Give me some more of your spent grain."

Three weeks later, the sorcerer comes back with a pack of mushrooms.

"Oh, but that is not magic," responds the beer brewer, "People have done this in the past, but now people want white button mushrooms from Paris, or chanterelles from the forest."

"White button mushrooms which grow on horse manure... and genetically modified chanterelles! Give me some more spent grain," said the sorcerer.

Six weeks later he came back with sausages.

"Oh, but that is not magic," responds the beer brewer, "Feeding cattle with spent grain and fattening up the pigs with it, and then making sausages from the waste of the pig, especially its blood - that has been done for centuries..."

"Pigs eat fish meal and they are fed their own bone meal, and pigs on antibiotics is what this is all about! Here I am offering you veggie sausages, made from mushrooms!"

"Vegetarian sausages? Having beer, bread, mushrooms and sausages - it sounds like we are ready for a very healthy Oktoberfest."

© 2002 Pauli

An Inspiration for Management:
PRODUCT PORTFOLIO

When we have market access and have built up a good distribution system, then we can broaden portfolio to access more purchasing power from the same customer. This improves market share and revenues, without increasing costs, through building on readily available markets, creating a very valuable the corporate brand. **One marketing channel can carry many products.**

These new products may all be made from the same core of raw materials. At first, it appears beer has little to do with mushrooms or bread, but once the entire package is assembled, whatever did not make sense from a marketing stand-point, could make greater production sense, leading to a much more efficient manufacturing system as well as optimizing resource management. An element of **surprise creates added consumer attention.**

Innovative product packages allow a change in the marketing message, from superficial slogans to a deeper emotional attachment… generating a customer loyalty unheard of before. Each product will have to perform in quality and price, but the combination of bringing new levels of efficiency into manufacturing and marketing makes it hard for others to match. **Create a product portfolio that offers depth.**

SHRIMP FARMING

The world market demand for shrimps is increasing rapidly. This crustacean offers a great price. In order to farm shrimps in an industrialized set-up to meet the increasing demands, meant an intervention in the natural environment of the shrimps, the mangroves. Shrimps thrived in mangroves, feeding on their natural food, algae. Mangroves were converted into basins to speed up the production process of shrimps. Mangroves used to dominate the coastal lines. The elimination of the mangroves eliminated the algae. The natural food of the shrimps is replaced by high protein concentrates: waste from slaughter houses. In order to increase efficiency, and profitability, the waste from the processing of the shrimps is now fed back to the shrimps. It also eliminates the need for extensive waste management. Since shrimps are not carnivores, neither cannibals, they cannot digest their own leftovers very well. This leads to a fast weight gain. Myth of productivity.

The feeding of shrimps with their own waste leads to a debilitation of the immune system which permits viral attacks. When the white spot virus attacks, all shrimps die in a few days. The traditional solution is based on the use of antibiotics and the genetic modification of shrimp larvae produced overseas in an artificially clean environment. The cost of production increases, the world supply goes up. When the virus attacked Ecuador, the prospect of US$750 million in exports evaporated in a few months. The economic crisis made it impossible for the "modern approach" based on hormones and genetic modification to be financed. Cash was lacking.

The solution was to carve out a niche, replanting the mangroves, which quickly bring back the natural nutrients, the algae. But once the ecosystem of the mangroves starts recovering, the bees will proliferate. The most productive centers of honey production are located in mangroves with each beehive generating up to 75 kg of honey whereas the average production is only a mere 7.5 to 10 kg. The production of honey, is then complemented with the generation of a very active and healthy propolis.

The waste from the shrimps (mainly chitin from which you can extract chitosan) is now recovered as an input for the production of natural band-aid, which, in combination with propolis, offers an all natural response to the regular need for health care. The ingredients to make these products are available in abundance, the cost of production is reduced and the price these shrimps and by-products command on the market is far superior to the standard products offered.

One channel can carry many products
Surprise attracts attention
A varied product portfolio creates depth

Let us see what our company really has when we put on the magic hat!

The Mushroom Chef

A cow is grazing and chews and chews the grass. In between the juicy grass, it finds a few mushrooms.

"Do not eat me!" screams the big mushroom, "I am making food for children."

"You are making food?" asks the cow with a sigh of disbelief. "I think you are just water and fiber. I am the one making food for kids!"

"That is all very well," says the mushroom, "we need your milk and meat, but please understand, I am more than just water and fiber. I actually contain a lot of goodies as well, perhaps as much as you."

"Impossible," replies the cow. "I produce milk all my life, and my meat is the best source of protein for the family."

"Yes, that is true, but it takes at least a year or two or more to turn you into a beef steak."

"So how long does it take before *you* can be harvested?"

"Two weeks!"

"No way, nothing grows in two weeks," replies the cow.

"Well as long as there is some waste, like your manure, or some straw and broken branches from trees, I can grow."

"Do you live off waste?"

"Whatever is left by plants and animals, we the fungi make it ready to be eaten again."

"I do not understand! You turn waste, including my waste, into food? Who wants *that*?"

"The truth is there is no such thing as waste in nature! I can make 1,000 times more protein per hectare per year, than you could ever generate with meat."

"This is a lie by 1,000 times!"

"Since I can be harvested every two weeks, and you every two years, and since you can only have two sisters living on one hectare, whereas I can have thousands, I can grow 1,000 times more food than you can!"

"That means I am not part of this food revolution?"

"Of course you are part of it. After I have grown my fruit, whatever is left is an excellent feed for you."

"That means you eat first, then I eat, and then both of us make enough food to stamp out hunger forever. How clever we are!"

© 2002 Pauli

An Inspiration for Management:
BOOSTING PRODUCTIVITY

An important tool for increasing competitiveness is through finding creative ways to improve productivity in existing product lines and processes. In past decades business tried to find productivity improvements, which has only marginally lead to lowering cost prices. The time has come to go beyond this, to look for the **productivity creating a cluster of industries**, not just of one product or process.

This leads to a search for innovative partnerships, because in a system one company alone cannot survive. The new partner need not be the one who has been on your radar screen in the past. These may be partners who have never been part of any of your core businesses, but who can surprisingly contribute remarkably well in responding to the needs of the customer in a way we could never have imagined. **These new partnerships maintain focus on the core business while embracing 'out of the box' thinking.**

At first, some of these partners may even seem small and irrelevant, but it is the discovery of the *unseen* and *unheard potentials* that lead to a new partnership, that is more effective in responding to the needs of the market. Having new partners may be fun. But having partners who are very different to you brings balance and diversity, which helps **to create new competitive systems.**

POROUS ASPHALT

Road construction and maintenance is a mature business. There are few innovations and the industry is driven by government contracts. When asphalt is deteriorating, it is scraped off, sent to a landfill and replaced by another cover of mixed bitumen and small rocks. The industry has not seen many innovations though it is faced with two problems: asphalt is a toxic waste and it is increasingly costly to dispose of, and does not drain rain so it creates a film which is dangerous for the drivers who can lose control due to hydroplaning (aquaplaning).

The solution is to produce porous asphalt. The problem is that most types of plastics which would permit permeability are recycled waste bottles made from PET or PE which melt in the production process of the asphalt, and this asphalt is subsequently more toxic than before. Whereas one is saving money at first, one is worsening the problem after the useful life of asphalt. The use of thermoplastics like polycarbonates is not feasible since it is too expensive and would make the road cover uneconomic.

Polycarbonates are in high demand. Their use ranges from casings for computers, covers for cell phones, security layers in windshields for cars and the main carriers of information on CDs and DVDs. Until recently, it was impossible to separate the thermoplastic from other layers of paper, aluminum and layers of magnetic stripes. Whereas each of the components is of high value on its own, as a mixture it is quite toxic. A new technology has been finetuned that allows the plastics to separate, thus creating a tremendous new supply of these valuable materials.

Now it is possible to imagine the production of porous asphalt with the best quality plastics, eliminating the toxicity of the road cover. This triggered another development - the recycling of porous asphalt which uses polycarbonates. Machinery has been developed to scrape off damaged asphalt, recondition it and use the same material on the spot as asphalt. This eliminates the need for landfill. It offers a direct use for used polycarbonates. It eliminates the need for transportation to the landfill and dramatically reduces the need for new asphalt, while creating a new concept of a road maintenance service at a lower cost, with an improved profitability, while launching a new machinery industry.

The Italian and the Japanese government are the first ones in the world to decide that all their roads have to be covered with porous asphalt. And both countries are cooperating through their local industries such as Hitachi, FIAT and ANAS on how to capitalize on this breakthrough that has been triggered, amongst others, thanks to a new technology in plastics recycling. Who would have guessed that road maintenance and plastics recycling had so much in common?

Productivity of a cluster of industries
Think out of the box while remaining focused on the core business
The market is driven through innovation

Let's grow mushrooms on waste and feed the world!

"Improved Cash Flow"

We love caffeine

A group of earthworms are working their way through a pile of organic waste.

"I need a rest," screams the old earthworm, "but I still feel so energized, so hyper!"

"I feel the same," cry his 1,000 babies, all born last month.

"How can we ever tell these people not to throw coffee or tea on the compost heaps?" asked the father earthworm.

"Exactly. They do not even like to drink coffee before they go to bed, so why do they throw all this caffeine into our faces? I am stressed out!" says the youngest of the colony.

"Well, what do I hear," wonders the shiitake mushroom, "you are all suffering from too much caffeine?"

"You see, people have learned they cannot feed cattle with coffee waste, because, although it is rich in nutrients, the cows get too stressed from caffeine, and give less milk!" says a worm.

"And since you do not give milk, people do not care?" enquires the shiitake mushroom.

"Well, they do not know what we are going through, but having to eat and digest your own weight every day is quite a job."

"I can help," says the shiitake. "I can grow here happily with my friends because I get my energy from the caffeine!"

"What? You get energy from caffeine without getting stressed?"

"No, actually the more caffeine there is, the better for me. I like to grow, converting the caffeine into food for others!"

"Wow, that would be great. But how does this work?"

"You are an animal, and coffee is a plant. I am a fungus, and we each belong to three different kingdoms."

"I know that even though we do not have legs and we are blind, we belong to the Animal Kingdom," says the earthworm proudly.

"So, animals suffer from caffeine, but some fungi can live off any fiber which includes caffeine. Then we produce waste, which is rich in protein, without caffeine."

"That is so clever! Fungi make food; earthworms prepare food for plants... and the cattle eats the plants. Everyone does their bit, and together we don't suffer from stress!"

© 2002 **Pauli**

An Inspiration for Management:
IMPROVING CASH FLOW

The objective of innovation is to respond better to market requirements. The market wants food. If one does this creatively, new products will emerge, using something we considered not even useless, caffeine was considered a problem. If one can identify new opportunities, like the shiitake farmed on caffeine-rich waste, then it will lead to better cash flow and the ultimate result is profitability.

The cash flow of an integrated business is higher than the cash flow of separate products.

The major drawback of any innovation is the risks involved in bringing change to the production process as well as to the market place. The only way to alleviate these risks is to ensure that there is a better cash flow. The conversion of hidden assets, on the basis of what is already available, using innovative technologies and efficient new forms of organization leads to **better cash flow, which reduces the risks involved.**

Innovation results in seeking creative angles in your business, which subsequently leads to lower risks. **The more innovation, the less risk.** This is a breakthrough for industry wishing to move on to new markets, which are stuck with less or even uncompetitive production systems.

GE PLASTICS AND POLYCARBONATES

The logic of recovering waste materials from one process as input for another are not limited to the organic world, as described in this tale. On the contrary, any process, including plastics, offer the same opportunity. One of the highest grade of plastics is the polycarbonate category. This heat-resistant material is highly popular for its use in the IT- and automotive industry, though the biggest recent demand comes from information carriers such as CDs, CD-R and DVDs. It is expected that this information storage medium for data, music and film will dramatically increase.

A CD is typically made out of a polycarbonate basis, an aluminum powder, gold and/or silver dust and some inks. Out of security, an increasing number of companies and government agencies wish to destroy the information prior to disposal since it includes sensitive data. And the capacity of these systems to store pictures, film and reports will increase dramatically over the next few years. The use of gold and silver warrants a high performance.

The design of CDs is a very high technological performance, though there is no consideration in the manufacturer's mind about the recycling of these materials into original components. The cost of disposing shredded CDs and related systems can be as low as US$20 per ton, and as high as US$150 per ton. Since General Electric is the largest producer of polycarbonates in the USA with some 35% of the market, they have an interest to maintain sales prices on par with production costs and the increased investment costs to maintain production in line with demand. At the same time, precious metals such as gold and silver should be recycled, and the risk of vinyl or chromium to be dispersed should be avoided.

The recycling of these materials permits the creation of a new influx of polycarbonates (PC) on the market. The simple separation of the components, thanks to a biological process, would lead to the availability of PC for other uses. Since the newly-obtained PC is reactive, it will permit its combination with other plastics that were not recyclable before. This creates a new market. The cost for separating the CDs can be as low as US$40 per ton. This leaves sufficient margin for the reception of all material, and the resale. Actually, with these prices one could even offer some of the high grade types of polycarbonates for free ... for specific uses such as sunglasses, which are completely made out of PC. A market characterized by scarce resources in a growing segment is now converted to one of abundance.

Innovation increases integrated cash flow
More cash flow reduces risk
More innovation facilitates less risk

Let us grow mushrooms on coffee, and feed cattle with the mushroom waste!

Who wants Red Rice?

A field full of rice is chattering away. There is a lot of discussion since a new family of rice will soon arrive. Instead of looking white, this rice would look red.

"That is impossible," screams the rice. "We have been white throughout our existence, why do people now want us to look red?"

"That is the price of progress," comments an algae floating around in a paddy full of water.

"Progress? How can you ever consider changing our natural color as progress? It's cosmetics!"

"No, it is progress! The people who you provide food for do not have enough healthy input anymore, and therefore what is missing has to become part of your genes."

"I have no idea what my genes are, but I do know that I have never ever seen a red rice-corn in my life, and I never want to!"

"Well, actually the 'red' is called beta-carotene and it's actually very good for people. If they eat this rice, they will never become blind."

"Oh I see! We have to look like a carrot so that people do not become blind!"

"Exactly! Actually, I have a lot of beta-carotene as well..." says the algae.

"YOU, you are rich in beta-carotene? You have to be joking, you have no red at all... you are as green as can be!"

"Well yes... but that is because I belong to the Kingdom of Algae, and you belong to the Kingdom of Plants."

"So why do I have to turn red, when you are my neighbor and you already have a lot of it in you?"

"Because I simply cannot produce enough beta-carotene, and children do not want to eat algae!"

"That's ridiculous. I have seen you around for as long as I can remember!"

"Yes, but there is too much wind, that is why I cannot grow."

"So why do people fumble around with my genes and make me red? Why don't they simply plant some bamboo to keep the wind away? Then we will have at least a hundred times more beta-whatever to make the blind see!"

© 2001 Pauli

An Inspiration for Management:
UNCOVER HIDDEN ASSETS

There are many opportunities to introduce innovation in your present business. If you do not have water, then you cannot farm any rice, but no one ever considered farming spirulina-algae in the abundant water of rice! Hidden assets are to be unearthed and once visible, these represent a solid new business line, and additional cash flow. **Hidden assets hold great potential for innovation.**

Once hidden assets are made visible, there is a need to find simple solutions to launch them into the marketplace. If innovations required substantial investments, it is risky in case they would not work. But it is so different when you can start with what you already have. **Hidden assets can be converted into cash flow with minimum expenditure** and little effort. One only has to realize what is readily available.

There are often solutions, which are more technological, and as such are considered more popular. However, management must remain open to finding the cheapest, fastest and least risky new ways of responding to market demand. Embarking on expensive technologies, which are perceived as more popular, are often less efficient and surplus to requirements. **Simple innovation, easy to implement with low capital input, are often more viable than expensive hi-tech.**

MALTING STATIONS

The world market for beer has consolidated over the years. This wave of mergers and acquisitions goes parallel with a less visible concentration of producers of malt, a key ingredient for beer. Barley for beer brewing needs to be malted, the seeds are left to germinate under controlled temperature and humidity and at the moment when the seeds start to sprout and have maximum starch content, the process is stopped abruptly through lowering temperature and moisture content. Once upon a time, all beer brewers had their malting station next door though the drive towards core business, and the need for a standardized product of a predictable quality lead to the externalization of malt. The brewer focused solely on the beer. This left hundreds of smaller malting stations idle.

As the malting market further consolidated, with numerous facilities closing in Eastern Europe, there is a vast amount of capital that stands idle, perhaps even forever. Whereas the malting station has no future for the making of malt, alternative uses could be imagined which make the best use of these installations which permit a perfect control of humidity and temperature levels. So the question is: which business could make use of this facility that is not part of the beer supply chain?

One of the industrial sectors which is undergoing a major transformation is the cattle-feed supply. Especially after the mad cow disease scare, it has become clear to producers, consumers and health authorities that the recycling of animal waste into the food cycle of the same animals is not permitted. The vast amounts of bone-meal are now incinerated for health reasons, and this created a new demand for better quality feed. The only option that has been quickly available is the supply of soya products, though there are other feed streams which can be used. For example, the waste from sugar beets, spent grain from the brewery, or straw from corn or wheat is not digestible for cattle, nor does it have the required nutrient content to satisfy the needs for a farmer.

If one were to process these agricultural left-overs from plant origin, and subject these to a fungal treatment, then the ligno-cellulose will be broken down and essential amino acids will be added. This process converts a low-quality feed into a high-quality grade with excellent nutritional value. The present price structure does not permit large investments in sophisticated installations. This is not necessary. The defunct malting stations are ideally equipped to offer this conversion of the feed industry, and the malting stations are available at face value. At a time when beer-brewers struggle to make ends meet, they may find surprise revenue in their spent grain, and a surprise return on an old malting unit that was discarded for years without ever imagining a possible return.

Hidden assets are the first priority
Convert hidden assets into cash flow
Simple and fast is often better than hi-tech

Let us eat spirulina algae with rice!

"Thinking Out of the Box"

Farming with Ocean Water

A strawberry and an asparagus are looking for a new place to live. They arrive along the coast of southern Africa and find rich soil. But there is no water.

"This soil is full of goodies, all we need is right here," claims the asparagus.

"Yes, but there is not a drop of water. We can't stay here."

"Come on, be positive! There is sun and sandy soil; the type we both like..." says the asparagus.

"The sun? You have it easy, you just grow deep in the sand, but my berries hang on the ground, I will have hot feet and burned cheeks," responds the strawberry.

"But we have the ocean right here, that will keep us cool!"

"You must be kidding, you know very well that salt water will kill us. Salt on soil destroys us forever."

"Is the ocean water warm or cold?" asks the asparagus. "Let's have a look." They discover the water is ice-cold.

"Brrrr, this must have come from the South Pole; it is way too cold for me!" screams the strawberry.

"The fact that it's cold is great! Just think: What happens when you have a cold glass of milk on the beach?"

"This is not fair. You make me thirsty and you know I cannot stand the thought of drinking salt water."

"Think before you answer please! What happens to a nice cold glass of milk on the beach?"

"It sweats."

"No, that's not sweat! It's called *condensation*."

"What is that?"

"There is always some water in the air, called humidity. If there is a lot of it, the air gets sticky. If there is too little, your skin dries out. So if we pump cold water through a pipe hanging above us, we will have all the water we need dripping down onto our leaves!"

"To have a shower like that, don't you need a pump?"

"No - the water will flow back to the sea as long as the pipe is lower at that end. And we'll have water forever."

"If it is so easy, let me have a second pipe along my roots so that I can have cold feet. That will make my berries very sweet."

© 2001 Pauli

An Inspiration for Management:
THINK OUT OF THE BOX

The first step to fostering creativity and innovation is to get your team to think 'out of the box'. It is not easy for someone, who has built a successful business and career on the basis of a proven product and existing technology, to drop all that is familiar to go in search of a new approach to the same business! **Once you get out of the box, you can get creative!**

Once management gets out of the box, it will see opportunities which are quickly visible to other 'out of the box' thinkers, and not at all relevant to those still in the box, operating in the protected atmosphere of 'past success' and 'proven track records'. Once creative ideas emerge, an exciting domino effect will occur, with more ideas leading to a breakthrough approach. **Once out of the box, new ideas lead to the redesign of a whole business model.**

New ideas will affect not only production, they will permeate all aspects, including costing, raw material supplies, quality management and opportunities to expand market demand, especially that of the original core product. **Innovation leads to market expansion of the core product, while thriving on new and efficient systems.**

BRITISH PETROLEUM AND CO_2

When the environment managers of BP discussed their strategies towards the Kyoto Protocol, voices quickly emerged requesting more funding for research. When one analyzes the type of research that the energy sector has invested in, one cannot deny a certain level of myopia. Nearly all funds dedicated to research are looking for the elimination of carbon dioxide, its storage into the deep sea or its sequestration by trees.

There are plans to pump it into the deep sea, representing billion dollar investments with doubtful results over time. The idea is that the oceans can absorb massive amounts of carbon dioxide. Another option is to use CO_2 to pump it into old wells and in the process extract more petroleum from these dying pits. Then there are proposals to engage in massive reforestation. The forestation that is considered is with trees, a strange option since trees are very slow in converting carbon dioxide into wood fibers. This is much better done through the planting of bamboo, which fixes up to 40 times more per hectare per year than a genetically-modified tree would ever be able to do.

Whereas each of the options considered are valid, the main problem is that none of the ones on the table actually consider CO_2 as a potential resource, which could add value. CO_2 is considered a problem which will cost money to get rid of. How can a business ever operate successfully and how can it create a new competitive edge when the solutions under consideration are not generating one penny of value added? This is not the right focus.

If a raw material is in abundance, then the products that can be created from it are potentially very cheap as well. Cheap products which respond to a real need and which represent a fundamental innovation could 'therefore" offer great market penetration. After all it demonstrates a unique selling proposition. If one looks at carbon dioxide, it has one carbon for every two oxygen molecules. Carbon is needed in numerous advanced materials. The carbon fiber is one of the priciest materials for the textile industry; a carbon-based car body has been announced as one of the future, and composite materials for the information technology industry is widely considered the wave of the future. What is the stumbling block? Cost!

The time has come to direct thousands of researchers towards finding creative uses for carbon. The oxygen molecule is no problem whatsoever; it has a guaranteed market in nature. The problem is that BP is not expected to get out of its core business, and therefore reverts to reducing the negative impact instead of searching for the innovations which will impact other sectors of the world economy.

'Out of the box'
Leads to increased creativity
One 'out of the box' idea leads to another...
'Out of the box' thinking secures market expansion

Let's begin farming strawberries and asparagus in the desert!

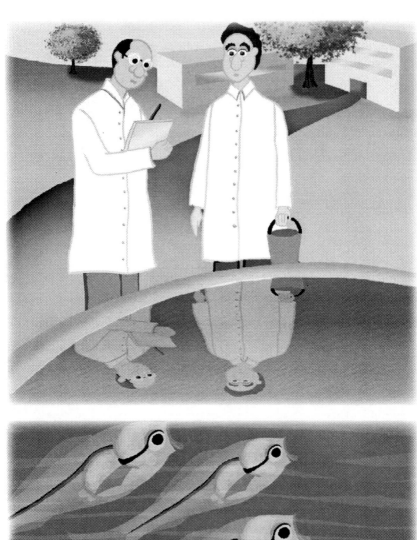

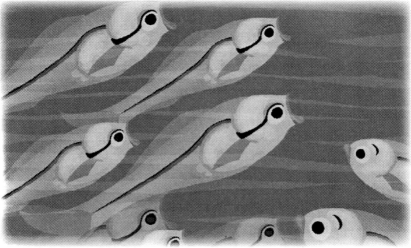

Males Only?

Thousands of young fish, called fingerlings, swim in an overpopulated pond. A few men in white approach the pond. All at once, the female fish starts to scream:

"Go and hide! Go and hide!"

"What is this all about?" asks their brother.

"Those men will spray hormones into our water!" they cry out loud.

"What is that? It sounds like horror on the moon!"

"Oh yes, these hormones are horrifying to us!"

"But what is it?"

"When males are growing up, at a certain age, they grow a beard. That's because their body is making male hormones. But we females have different hormones."

"Sure, but what is wrong with the men in white giving us hormones?"

"They only put *male* hormones in the pond. And we females do not want to have beards!"

"Ha – ha – ha! Females having beards, that is funny... then you wouldn't be girls anymore!"

"Exactly! We are not screaming out of hysteria, this is a matter of survival for us!"

"Do you mean that these men in white put hormones into the water that make you male?"

"Yes!" scream the ladies.

"Why would they want to do such a stupid thing? It would be no fun to only have males in this overcrowded pond."

"Because they do not want our eggs and babies!"

"No more babies? But how can we survive if we cannot have offspring?"

"Humans only want to produce food for mankind, and since we need energy to make eggs, which have no time to hatch, we females produce less meat for the same cost."

"But what happens to a pond that is overflowing with males?"

"If there are only males in the pond, then the same men in white will have to add antibiotics to keep illnesses away!"

"But who on Earth wants to eat food full of hormones and antibiotics? That doesn't sound tasty!"

"And just think – if *we* are full of hormones and antibiotics, and the men in white eat us, then what happens to *them*?"

© 2001 Pauli

An Inspiration for Management:
DIRECTING RESEARCH & DEVELOPMENT

The drive to increase productivity and the desire to bring more products to market faster may tempt us to go beyond the limits of nature. Science must remain within natural systems, which have evolved over billions of years. Changing female fish into males is not a sign of creativity, but rather an aberration of creativity. **R&D searches for the most creative solutions within existing ecosystems.**

If we can increase productivity of the land in terms of the production of amino acids with a factor 1,000, why would we ever consider genetically manipulating plants or fish? When we can grow spirulina algae in the wastewater of rice, why would we ever consider genetically manipulating rice to include the nutrients of spirulina? **There is immense room for breakthroughs within existing ecosystems.**

Billions of people suffer from unmet basic needs, while billions of tons of 'waste' are squandered. Clearly, updating is overdue. We must remain on the path of progress, which ultimately responds to people's needs *in co-evolution with nature*. **R&D, in co-evolution with nature, offers thousands of opportunities unheard of before.**

PANASONIC AND VARTA BATTERIES

Batteries are a part of modern life. How could we imagine operating a cellphone, a game-boy, a laptop computer or a watch without a battery? The batteries are able to respond to the need for mobility and independence from the electric grid. Though we are well aware of the advantages batteries offer to us, we are also aware of the clear dangers the dispersion of wasted batteries represents to our health.

Batteries are made out of metals, heavy metals which are known to cause cancer. The makers are very well aware of the risks involved and therefore have substituted the highly toxic components with less noxious types. That is a major step forward but all batteries still depend on the use of metals, heavy metals in particular. The second response to this imminent danger has been the installation of aggressive campaigns to secure the full recycling of all batteries. In spite of the great efforts undertaken by the government, there is no country that seems to succeed in gathering more than 75% of the batteries that get distributed. An amazing 25% remains a danger to our environment and our health.

A South African company (Freeplay) identified a niche in the market; since no one was able to even afford the batteries, they designed a lamp and a radio with energy generated through the turning of a crank. It works well and has forced other radio and lamp producers to follow suit. But the battery makers of the world remained unmoved by this development. The creation of bio-batteries has been discussed by some researchers and this offers a great perspective. But what better than to imagine a battery that after its use can simply be thrown on the compost heap?

The inspiration comes from the whale. This wonderful mammal generates some six volts of energy through the reaction of potassium and calcium and it pumps some 1,000 liters per pulse. This is a most efficient generation of energy and an impressive transmission of energy into pumping power. All mammals are able to generate electricity in a comparable fashion and therefore it is astonishing that the most sustainable way of energy production has been off the research charts of Varta and Panasonic, two of the leading makers of batteries around the world. After all, a child living in a favela in Latin America may not be able to afford a game-boy, nor the batteries, but that child does have access to banana peels (potassium) and egg shells (calcium) and could one day invent the bio-battery of the future.

R&D within ecosystems
Opportunities are unlimited
R&D in co-evolution with nature

Let us make certain that hormones don't play with women's beards!

"Choose Appropriate Technologies"

Why Can't I Eat Sugar?

Mr. Tree meets Mrs. Sugarcane, with tears in her eyes.

"How are you?" asks Mr. Tree.

"I am not happy," whispers Mrs. Sugarcane.

"I can see that, but why, my friend?" responds the tree.

"Because people only want the worst of me, my sugar and nothing else."

"Sugar is bad for teeth and makes people gain weight. But what is it you have that is good?"

"Fiber ... I have a lot of fiber, but people burn it."

"You are rich in fiber? No, no, it is me, the tree who is the world's supplier of fiber which is made into paper and packaging."

"And how long does it take for you to grow this fiber?"

"It takes me 20 years to grow, and fiber makes up 20% of me," responds the tree proudly.

"Well! I grow in less than ONE year, and fiber makes up 80% of me! So why don't they make paper out of me?" argues the sugarcane.

"Perhaps because they do not know about sugarcane in Canada or Sweden where most of the paper mills are! Now come to think of it - I have a lot of sugar too..."

"You, the tree, you have sugar?"

"Yes... actually 30% of me can be converted to sweet sugars which do *not* attack teeth, and do *not* cause weight gain."

"So what do people do with your sugar now?"

"Oh, they burn it when making paper."

"How ridiculous!"

"Yes, and worse still, since they want more fiber faster, they have even manipulated my genes so that trees can be harvested in only 10 years, instead of 20!"

"At least they still utilize *you*. It is worse for me! In order to have sweets, they now make *synthetic* sugars!"

"Gosh – people would have happier kids if they made sweets from the tree ... and if they made paper from sugarcane!"

"Then people could enjoy a lot of sweets, and have more paper to read and draw with.... *without* getting cavities and destroying the forests. Then we could all be happy!"

© **2001 Pauli**

An Inspiration for Management:
CHOOSE APPROPRIATE TECHNOLOGIES

We have to direct our attention towards new technologies that make sense. If management is to be kept on the tips of its toes then it needs to build in some form of discontinuity when taking products and processes forward. In order to see the new chances that are elsewhere, one can imagine the same end product responding to the same need but using local resources creatively. **Discontinuity stimulates creativity.**

Business may first search to replicate proven models from elsewhere. Paper is made from pine and eucalyptus trees all around the world, but when you are in the tropics, these resources are simply not available. Planting eucalyptus and pine trees in the tropics does not make sense. The richest source of fibers is sugar cane. Extracting fiber from bagasse, the waste from sugarcane, cannot be obtained using the same technologies as used for extracting fibers from a tree. This requires a different technology. **The same product made from different raw materials requires different technologies.**

Insisting on the use of a process technology that one controls will lead to disconnection with the local market over time. Clients welcome respect for biodiversity, and enjoy quality products at competitive prices, using technologies adapted to this new environment. **Innovation requires flexibility.**

ASK BOARD (INDONESIA)

The market for roof material has been dominated for decades by fiber cement. It is cheap, locally produced, long-lasting and functional. The joints are easy to make, the bolting down on a roof structure is quickly done. There is no doubt about it, the fiber has outstanding properties. A mere three percent blend with cement offers a resistance to pressure that is unmatched. The only problem it has is the use of a mineral fiber that gives the strength to cement, known as asbestos.

Asbestos is cheap and mined in Canada and Russia, but unfortunately is fatal when the airborne dust accumulates in the lungs, leading to many respiratory ailments. Companies have been sued for billions of dollars over the havoc created by asbestos. The product is now forbidden in many countries, though Third World countries it is still widely used mainly because of cheaper costs.

Whereas asbestos is a naturally-occurring mineral, its substitutes today are mainly synthetic, i.e. derived from petrochemicals. Their performance is close to that of asbestos, though the cost is considerably higher. There are natural alternatives to these fibers, but these are considered too expensive. There is one additional problem: in order for natural fibers to be used, one must make certain that no residual sugars remain in the mix, otherwise the cement will not crystallize.

These problems have bogged down the natural substitutes to asbestos. ASK Board, a Japanese company, successfully undertook to replace asbestos and the asbestos substitutes with bamboo fibers. Thanks to the planting of some 2,000 hectares of bamboo, ample local supply is guaranteed with little need for transport. The production plant is located outside Jakarta and produces a cement board reinforced with bamboo fibers. The first surprise is that instead of the typical grey look, a roof covered with ASK Board has a distinctive green shade. It is pleasant to watch and – more important – it is comfortable to live in since the green reflects the sun. The second surprise is the carbon dioxide balance. Indeed, the cement board reinforced with bamboo requires about 50% bamboo, compared to only 3% asbestos. This increases the long-time use of bamboo that effectively sequesters the carbon dioxide.

Discontinuity stimulates creativity
The same product – different raw material –
New technologies
Innovation requires flexibility

Let's use sugar from the tree!

"Re-engineering"

How to take it apart?

A big elephant sits sadly gazing at the horizon, when a chimpanzee swings by and says:

"What is wrong with you? You are healthy, young, admired and you are one of the five wise animals."

"Ah, I would like to be able to use my fingers, especially my thumb. Why don't I have fingers like you?"

"Because you have a strong and powerful trunk instead, which can pluck leaves from high up in the trees. What do you need fingers for?"

"I would like to ride a bicycle."

"A bicycle? Are you crazy, bicycles are not made for big animals like you!"

"Oh yes they can be. There is a big one made for the circus, but I cannot ride it."

"Why - is it not strong enough?"

"Yes, it's strong enough, but since I am so big and heavy, I need to be able to ring the bell to announce I am coming, so people can get out of the way."

"But you can blow your trunk instead and make a sound like a trumpet!"

"No, I don't want to blow my trunk - I want to be able to ring the bell like you and everyone else can. I want to ring the bell with a thumb, but I do not have one."

"Look, people have fingers, and I have fingers too, but you are compensated with a trunk instead."

"Do you want my trunk in exchange for your fingers?"

"No, silly, that isn't possible. And anyway, why are you so fascinated by people?"

"Because they have fingers and know how to put things together. They are smart."

"What do you mean - *smart*? The only smart ones are their kids. It takes them hours and days to put something together, but they take it apart in minutes, even seconds!"

"And the adults?"

"They only know how to put things together. They have no clue how to take it apart. Worse still, if they have no idea what to do with the stuff after use or when it breaks, they either throw it away or burn it with fire!"

"Fire! That is something we never use. It could kill us all. I am so glad I am not considered *intelligent*... I do not even know how to make fire!"

© 2001 Pauli

An Inspiration for Management:
REDISCOVER RE-ENGINEERING

If we wish to rethink our industrial processes and overhaul the engineering in order to regain the success which is fading or has been lost, then we need to ask ourselves what kind of innovation are we pursuing. Are we introducing yet another version of the same, or are we really rethinking how we do business? **Re-engineering requires getting to the core of a business.**

Once you realize what your core business is, and what the weaknesses are of other players in the market, then you can imagine that what may *appear* to be one of your weaknesses, can easily be converted into one of your strengths. This requires you to revisit the way you see yourself, and the way you appreciate other successes in the market. **Most successes have a weakness.**

If your business is in distress, search for a turn-around using what you already have. If your business is a success, look even closer to what you have already built up, because it will be faster and cheaper to build up a fresh competitive edge with hidden assets, than to resort to outside solutions. The key is to focus on your present weaknesses and alleviate those, since the competition will quickly gain market share by simply tackling your shortcomings and converting these into their strengths. **Do better with what you already do best.**

TETRA PAK

The invention of aseptic packaging was a breakthrough on the milk market. The innovation was revolutionary. It saved energy since the introduction of this multi-layered packaging allowed for the packaging, transportation and storage of milk for a long duration without the need for any refrigeration. The invention was so revolutionary that it quickly gained a leading position in the market for milk, juices and, later on, many other liquid products such as wine, coffee and yoghurt.

At first the product emerged out of concern for shelf life and energy savings, while securing the best hygienic conditions. Environmental concerns started to question the logic of this solution. The Life Cycle Analysis (LCA) for drinks places this solution at the fourth (and last) position after PET bottles, aluminum cans and glass bottles. The reason is the incapability of the company to recover the thin aluminum layer that is at the core of the technology.

The aseptic packaging, as the Tetra Pak system is known, consists of a layer of aluminum, sandwiched between two layers of low density poly-ethylene, and a cover made from paper and cardboard. Whereas Tetra Pak has designed an ingenious system to create this multilayered packaging system under a vacuum, it has not been able to separate the distinct components.

Research has indicated that the aluminum foil of a one-litre packaging brick has energy stored which is the equivalent of three hours of viewing TV. This energy is simply lost if the package is discarded ending up in a landfill, or is incinerated. Tetra Pak has invested in a research program to try to recover the aluminum but has been incapable of succeeding in the process.

As soon as Tetra Pak is able to separate the aluminum and recover this nearly-pure, non-ferrous metal, it will become the best performer on the LCA score. In the meantime, the product and packaging system is still very profitable, but losing marketshare and is under pressure to respond to a growing demand not to squander limited resources through "a once only use" of a resource that leaves a major footprint on the Earth.

Re-engineer around the core business
Every success has a weakness – find it
Convert weaknesses into strengths

Let us be happy to have no need to make a fire!

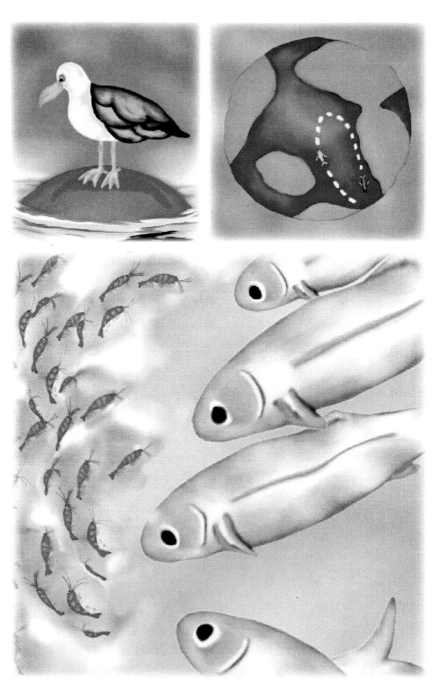

"Understand Your Reasons for Success"

The King of Hearts

A baby whale meets a seagull in the ocean and asks: "How can you fly so far away from land?"

"It's easy. I have wings and when I am tired, I just hang in the air, against the wind, rest and fly."

"But don't you fall down?"

"No, I do not fall down, I have wings - I fly."

"But isn't there gravity, this magnet from the Earth which pulls you down to the ground?" asks the baby whale.

"That's a good point, but not completely true. If I close my wings, I will drop like a stone, but if I keep them open, energy from the wind will support me."

"How sad I do not have wings. I would like to fly."

"You do not need wings, you can swim *and* you have a great heart."

"All of us have a heart and you have a small heart. But I do not even have small wings; I cannot even fly a little."

"Whales have the biggest hearts in the world. You are so big and strong - and yet you are so kind."

"Oh yes, that is true. Mom says my heart will do a great job as long as I eat well. I will be able to grow as big as my dad."

"How big is your heart?"

"I do not know; mom says that soon I will pump 200 litres with each heart beat. Daddy even pumps 1,000 litres per beat!"

"You are so big and so strong, yet you never eat meat, fruits or veggies. Why?"

"Most of us eat tasty krill which gives us a lot of energy so that we can grow, and even make electricity."

"You are joking! I know you can talk to each other from the North Pole to the South Pole when you sing together, but making electricity? Impossible!" laughs the seagull.

"What do you think makes the heart beat? It is an electric shock."

"What? Electricity makes your heart beat. Mine too?"

"Any heart."

"And how does this work?" questions the seagull, who is now getting very interested.

"We have these two elements in our body, they react, make electric impulses, then our muscles contract and so we pump the blood."

"Fantastic, so I can fly ... and I make electricity, and you, you could power a lighthouse!"

© 2001 Pauli

An Inspiration for Management:
YOUR REASONS FOR SUCCESS

If you see others who are successful, just be inspired, but do not imitate what seems to work for them. Instead, understand what works for you. Success is very specific to your business, your market, your culture, tradition and *you*. In this way, others will find it very difficult to imitate you. **Different successes have different reasons for being successful.**

If you wish to sustain your success, then you have to understand how you became successful. Your new product or service may become a hit, but what really made it a hit is not the result of just one factor, it is the interplay of many factors: the right product at the right time and place. **Understand your systems of success,** so that when the time and place changes, you can act and adapt, securing continuity of your leadership.

Once you grasp the reasons for your success, you can begin a never-ending process of improving each element that made you gain such a leading position in the first place. Before jumping into something new, embark on a never-ending exercise whereby you **strive to do better at what you already do best.** This is the most certain way to cut costs, improve margins and to build up market share. You will spread yourself too thin jumping too fast into a search for another new success, without nurturing and building on what you already have.

GOLDEN HOPE (MALAYSIA)

The demand for palm oil is rising globally. Its first and foremost use is as a vegetable oil for cooking, the second use is the extraction of laurel ether sulphate (LES) as a core ingredient for biodegradable soaps. The management of the plantations is a major challenge since the increased demand for oil has lead to a clearing of the tropical rainforest and subsequent reduction of the habitat of wildlife, including the orangutan, an endangered primate.

Malaysia is the largest producer of palm oil and its derivatives in the world. The plantations are decades old and are located around to Kuala Lumpur, the capital of Malaysia. The extraction of the oil from the fruits requires an integrated harvesting and processing scheme which is based on a just-in-time system that has proven its effectiveness over the years. First the leaves are removed and subsequently the fruits are harvested and shipped straight to the factory. All the fruits are subjected to a steam bath aimed at stopping further fermentation of the fruits, and the elimination of insects. Whereas this is a standard procedure around the world, this treatment leads to the elimination of Vitamin E.

Vitamin E is a much sought after ingredient for the cosmetics and the food industry. Demand is so high that prices increased and the production of a synthetic alternative has filled the gap between supply and demand for natural ones. Whereas the synthetic Vitamin E now dominates the market, it is fact that this variety is not as effective as the natural ones though in view of the costs involved, very little could be done. That is until Golden Hope took the initiative as the first palm oil producer to adapt the extraction process to secure the isolation of Vitamin E.

Whereas Vitamin E is not part of the core business, the high incidence of this valuable ingredient made the board decide to exploit this opportunity. Based on an Italian production engineering design, Golden Hope is now recovering the valuable component, which is sold on the open market to the highest bidder. This is a valuable first step. A second step is the recovery of the beta-carotene, another coveted ingredient. The market for vegetable oils prefers the golden look of corn (maize) oil. The red color of the beta-carotene is now masked with the addition of color pigments. The solution would be to extract the beta-carotene and sell it on the market, saving money since one avoids the use of color pigments, making money by offering a valuable ingredient to the personal care market at a competitive price.

Different successes for different reasons
Understand your system for success
Strive to do better at
What you already do best

Let's make electricity from banana peels and fish bones.

Market Research

Growing Coffee in Paris

Carlos from Colombia goes to Paris to teach the French how to grow coffee.

His market study confirms that the French drink a lot of coffee.

"But," asks the French businessman, "do we have the right climate for coffee like you have in the tropics?"

"No, but no problem. We will build a small green house and imitate our tropical climate with temperature and humidity control. Then you can grow coffee in Paris," says Carlos.

"But," murmurs the Frenchman, "we do not have the right soil; ours is thick and sticky, how can you grow coffee here? Don't you need volcanic soil?"

"No problem, we can ship you all the soil you need by boat."

"But," questions the Frenchman, "we have no seeds, and lack the experience."

"No problem. Next time you have a holiday, come to Colombia... spend a week in Cartagena on the beach, and then visit us in the Coffee Region and we will teach you everything you need to know about farming coffee."

The Frenchman thinks the Colombian is crazy.

A few weeks later a Frenchman called Jean goes to Bogotá to show the Colombians how to grow *Champignons de Paris*, also known as white button mushrooms.

His market studies confirm that Colombians eat a lot of white mushrooms. So they should grow these themselves.

"But," says the Colombian businessman, "do we have the right climate? Isn't it too hot here?"

"Yes, but no problem. We can build a small house and imitate our cold humid climate, all with automatic controls," says Jean.

"But," murmurs the Colombian, "we do not have the right soil, ours is volcanic, and for white mushrooms I have been told you need a lot of horse manure."

"No problem, we can ship you all the horse manure you need."

"But," questions the Colombian, "we have no seeds, and lack the experience."

"No problem. Next time you have a holiday, come to Paris... spend a week in the south of France, and afterwards visit us, and we will teach you everything you need to know."

The Colombians think it must be a good business and invest.

A few years later, he goes bankrupt since he could not compete. The banks blame low labor productivity for their failed investment.

© 1997 Pauli

An Inspiration for Management:
MARKET RESEARCH

Whenever you want to chart new territories and undertake market research, make sure you are cautious about your conclusions. There are a lot of subjective interpretations. You need to study the market from the *local* point of view, and not from the hard sales angle required to meet the bottom-line back home. **Market research should bring you closer to new customers through local support.**

If you wish to respond to local markets, then it would be possible to find similar solutions that could thrive on the local diversity. For example, instead of growing white button mushrooms for which everything needs to be changed, why not use the existing rich biodiversity which gives you tasty shiitake mushrooms which not only command a better price, there is also less competition than with white mushrooms. **Local systems closer to the market bring higher returns.**

Once the core business of mushrooms has been introduced, and innovations have been identified - creating better margins by using what is locally available - then one could even export the best back home. **A higher return overseas brings innovation back home.**

PULP AND PAPER IN BRAZIL

The pulp and paper industry is based on a standard raw material: pine or eucalyptus tree. The production process, which evolved from Scandinavia, North America and Japan, is highly capital intensive. When the industry expanded around the world and demand for paper increased, the production capacity had to rise in tandem with an increase in supply of raw materials. Since the logging of primary forests had caused major devastation, and the farming of trees imposed itself, it offered an opportunity to standardize the whole process.

In line with supply chain management, the forestry sector opted for species from the northern hemisphere as the standard on the market. Trees were gradually improved up to the point that, thanks to the favorable climatology and soil conditions, a eucalyptus tree would grow to maturity for harvesting in about 7 years. Local research confirmed that this was the best and fastest growth conditions ever encountered. The forestry industry therefore decided in coordination with the pulp and paper sector, to dramatically expand in China and Brazil.

The market research identified other sources of fibers, like straw from rice, bagasse from sugar cane and bamboo, as possible sources. These were available in abundance, though the patented technological process of de-lignification of woods such as eucalyptus and pine trees produces predictable length and strength of fibers. The same technology, applied to these new fiber sources would simply not generate the same type of quality of fibers. As a result, the abundant resources were discarded and the forestry companies embarked on a massive campaign to create forests with non-native and improved species.

This certainly makes sense for the corporation that controls the alkali sulfate technologies; it improves the return on existing capital investments, including intellectual property rights. On the other hand, it opens the market for newcomers who see this opportunity. They are prepared to take the local materials which are offered at much lower cost, change the process technologies so that the fibers meet the parameters set forth by the paper makers, and as such offer an alternative to the introduction of foreign species which is bound to lead to a long-term reaction against the companies. The first bamboo paper company in Brazil is operating at full capacity. Mitsubishi Paper (Japan) and Kymmene (Finland) have no way to respond to this niche strategy. But if they were prepared to adjust their process technologies and their northern hemisphere typology of sources of fibers, then they would be able to change the competitive game on the market. They have yet to decide to do this.

**Market research must bring you closer
to the local market
The closer you are to the market,
the higher your return
Higher returns overseas
bring innovations home**

*Let us not farm coffee in Paris
just because the French drink coffee!*

Local Expertise

Drinking in the Desert

A young mouse is visiting a faraway relative in the African desert. It is hot, and after a long trip, he finally arrives.

"I can hardly walk on the sand," says the young adventurer, "it is too hot for my feet."

"Well," says uncle who is happy to finally see a relative, "just lick your feet, then they will stay cool."

"Lick my feet! You have to be joking. My tongue is so dry, because I am thirsty and I do not have enough saliva. Look – I can't even spit!"

"Thirsty are you? Well then let's go and chew on the *Welwitschia*."

"The *well*, how can you chew on a *well*?"

"No, no, there is no well here in the desert, I speak of a very dear friend, the **Welwitschia...**"

"Booh, a witch, how can you get a drink from a witch?"

"There is no 'well' and there is no 'witch'. The *Welwitschia* is a plant!"

"There are no plants growing in the desert, otherwise this would not be called a desert!" snaps the hot mouse.

"That is what *you* believe up there in the jungle, but here *are* plants, and this one makes a great juice," replies the uncle.

"We have apple juice, orange juice, or juice from leaves in the jungle. But here I'll just settle for water. I am thirsty! There is no rain or river in this desert – how do you *survive*?"

"The *Welwitschia* harvests the morning dew."

"Morning dew ... the air here is so dry I can hardly breathe!"

"Every day in the morning, thanks to the cool night, there is dew. The *Welwitschia* is smart and collects the drops of dew and that is enough for us to live off."

"But why do you have to chew then, why don't you just *lick* the dew?"

"Because I want the nutrients, the minerals, the vitamins, all these goodies are made by the same plant. So I chew on its long leaves and I get it all in one go for free!"

"But if I were to chew on *your* feet, it would hurt; you'd get an infection and may even die!"

"That is true with animals, but chewing these leaves actually makes this plant even stronger. And since the *Welwitschia* is our only source of water in the desert - *everyone* chews on her."

"Brrrrr, I would rather die than be chewed on alive."

"The *Welwitschia* loves to be chewed on. She is now the oldest plant on earth, thanks to us chewing on her!"

© **2001 Pauli**

An Inspiration for Management:
LOCAL EXPERTISE

If you are in a business that is ready to operate outside national boundaries, you need local expertise. **Local input means getting closer to your customers.** All too often we just bring a global standard to local markets, and forget that whatever works for us back home, may simply not work elsewhere. Of course one needs to roll out procedures and unified reporting schemes, but so much is different and new that we have to listen to local voices.

At the same time, by observing and doing as the Romans do in Rome, offers inspiration and new ideas for innovation back home. Indeed, it gives insights that we never had before, and a vision that whatever we do well at home, can also be done better elsewhere, giving us a unique edge. **Responding successfully to local clients overseas means innovation back home.**

Companies want to be local yet global. This demands adaptability to local reality. And since adaptation means flexibility, which usually leads to innovation, the combination makes your business more competitive. **Flexibility means competitiveness.**

BROOKE BOND'S COMMITMENT TO RENEWABLE ENERGY

Brooke Bond is one of the world's largest tea plantations. Twenty years ago it was acquired by the Unilever conglomerate which includes food, home and personal care products. The famous Lipton Tea brand that produces some 80 billion tea bags each year sources much of its tea from this plantation. The supply of tea is guaranteed through a meticulous supply system which includes plantations in India, Kenya and Tanzania. The plantation in Kericho, Kenya, started in 1924 with the bushes still generating quality tea leaves.

Brooke Bond adheres to some strict environmental principles, including the refusal to expand farming land through the clearing of primary forests, and the maximum possible use of renewable energy. This has lead to the decision by the management in Kenya to opt for hydropower stations which have been in operation for over half a century (and still going strong) and the use of old steam boilers (recycled rail locomotives) to generate steam burning wood. As the supply of firewood poses a major challenge, Brooke Bond decided to embark on the planting of a fast-growing eucalyptus variety. In total some 3,000 ha of farmland of the tea plantation have been reserved for that purpose.

Eucalyptus trees grow quickly to maturity. In about seven years, the newly-planted tree will have reached a size ready for harvesting. Whereas the energy content of eucalyptus is well established on an international scale, a local bamboo species emerged as a possible substitute. Whereas bamboo can never compete with eucalyptus on a kilogram-per-kilogram basis, nor it's derived energy (since it is empty on the inside), bamboo does outperform eucalyptus when one makes a three-thronged calculus: how much energy can be derived per hectare per year. Indeed, bamboo is a grass, and can already be harvested less than three years after planting. Each year, for the following 70 years, bamboo will keep on providing culms. The "emptiness" is solved through the production of charcoal which reduces the volume and weight, while increasing the calorific value of the bamboo, surpassing the value of eucalyptus.

The potential energy generation from native bamboo is so strong that one could imagine the scaling back of the amount of land reserved for tree plantations to one third. As such, the Brooke Bond plantation in Kenya will increase its output of tea, without ever needing additional land, or having to clear a forest. Since there is native bamboo in over 100 countries around the world, these local solutions with local species could make a substantial contribution to the overall sustainability of a corporation like Brooke Bond.

The more local interaction, the closer you become to the market
The closer you are to the market, the more innovation for back home
Adapting locally makes you competitive globally

Let us learn
how to chew leaves in the desert!

The Ant Farmer

A lion is walking through the Savannah, and he looks around him at all the animals in his Kingdom. There is a lot of food, and everyone lives in paradise. Only the ants keep running around, acting so busy.

The King decides to visit the ants' nest. Hundreds, perhaps thousands, or even millions of ants run around like crazy.

"Hey, hey, hey, stop for a moment please, I am King of the Animals."

The ants do not seem to hear, or care, and continue running around, up and down, in and out of their nest, hoisting leaves.

The King Lion decides to scratch the ground, and before he knows it, hundreds of ants climb into his paw, and sting him.

"Aw! That hurts, you little beggars, you are so small I cannot even see you under my fur!"

A turtle walks by and says to the King Lion: "With all due respect, Sire, please do not disturb the ants, they are busy farming."

"Ants, are not farmers," replies the King Lion, "I never saw them harvesting grain or veggies. They don't eat that stuff!"

"Well, Sire, they do not farm plants, they farm *mushrooms*."

"Mushroom farming is for people, no animal knows how to do that!"

"Not true, Sire. Ants and termites are perhaps the best and the first farmers in the world."

"But how can they ever farm in the dark below the ground? Don't they need light and air, water and fertilizer?"

"Indeed - the queen brings a bit of fungi with her, and in her nest, she makes the best food for the fungi, so they love to grow there next to her."

"I do not understand; if the ants make food for the fungi, where do they get the food for the fungi in the first place?"

"Ants collect edible waste, and if there is not enough waste, they get some leaves, chew them up and make moist pasta."

"Pasta? I thought this came from China, or Italy?"

"Sire, this is a different pasta and the fungi love it, they grow on it and then the ants eat the fungi which continue to grow and never dies."

"Ants seem to have to run all the time to get a nice dinner. I prefer to go hunting, have a good chase ending in a tackle - and the meal is ready!"

© 2000 Pauli

An Inspiration for Management:
CORE COMPETENCE

Management needs to understand the core competence of its own corporation as well as that of its competition. There are core competencies that we seldom identify. We need to search for them, since it is a pre-condition for understanding how to stimulate more innovations. For instance, mushroom-farming is the core competence of the ants, although even the King did  not know or understand that initially. **Mastering core competencies is the basis for new innovations.**

Other core competencies may be around in the market, but it becomes apparent only when you realize it. Mankind always thought he was the first farmer, only to realize that ants have been farming long before us and actually has the strongest farming system on Earth. **Look at the core competence identifying who is better than you out of your traditional market.**

The study of core competence leads to the identification of new ways of doing business. It makes us look beyond the obvious since we never realized or identified that ants are mushroom farmers. In fact, they are not only mushroom farmers, they are the greatest fertilizers of top soil, feeding 1,000,000 ants for every human being on Earth ... *without* ever triggering traffic jams! **Studying core competencies leads to "out of the box" innovation.**

Storm Brewery in St.John, Newfoundland, Canada

When Michael McBride decided to start his own brewery, he realized that microbreweries had a hard time competing on price with the market leader Labatt. On the other hand, the quality of his beer was so superior that he expected it to take the market by storm and he called his brewery Storm Brewery. Though the market for quality beer at double and triple the price is marginal, being a brew master, he wanted to dedicate to the making of an outstanding product. But he quickly realized that his chance of surviving the market was slim unless he found another revenue stream.

The core competence of a beer brewer is the art and science of converting barley (worth) with water, yeast and hops into a delightful beverage. The core of the technique depends on the mastering of the fermentation process, which traditionally takes 21 days. The brewer who adheres to the German Purity Principle (Reinheitsgebot) is stuck with a competitive disadvantage over the large-scale brewers since they use enzymes to speed up the fermentation that will be limited to a mere 2 days. Saving 19 days of storage (and cash) secures a major cost advantage. Well aware of this challenge, Michael set out to find another revenue stream but his bankers urged him to stick to his core business based on his core competence.

A master beer brewer is really an expert in micro-biology. Handling yeast, a single cell fungus, requires knowledge in handling environmental conditions, which lead to the fermentation of all ingredients into a predictable taste, with a well-defined color and a typical foam. When searching the Internet, Michael found out about an experiment in Namibia, undertaken by the ZERI Foundation, to farm mushrooms in the Namibian desert using spent grain and local elephant grass. He decided to see for himself. Seeing is believing.

Michael realized that his core competence as a master beer-brewer suited him ideally as a master mushroom farmer. He quickly embarked on a mushroom farming exercise whereby, he noted that the heat generated from the fermentation process offered cheap energy to keep his mushroom operation going through the cold winter. The acidic water from the cleaning process could be used to sterilize the spent grain prior to the inoculation with mushrooms and when Michael put all elements together he realized that a beer-brewer had everything needed to become a mushroom farmer. Now he sells beer and mushrooms, offering a double cash flow and all is based on his core business and core competencies. It improves his competitive position vs. Labbatt on the local market, and strengthens his standing in the Newfoundland community.

Know your core competence
Study core competence of the best - especially if they are not in your business
"Out of the box" core competence stimulates your innovation

Let us farm mushrooms from the inside out, like the ants!

"Diversification"

Forests secure drinking water

A deer sips fresh water from a wonderful little creek flowing through the forest.

"I recall having a drink here years ago and I had terrible diarrhea afterwards," the deer comments to a squirrel jumping around in a nearby tree.

"You are right. A decade ago nothing grew here and everyone left because they got sick from the bad water," squeaks the squirrel.

"Why didn't people dig a well and pump water up from the ground?"

"They may have tried but perhaps it didn't work. Pumps need parts and energy and often these pumps break down. Meanwhile, there was an urgent need to have water for everyone all the time," said the squirrel.

"But if children were dying, why didn't they bring water from the big city?" asks the deer.

"That was too expensive. Instead of sending water here, people had to go to where the water was, miles and miles away. And no one stayed behind."

"Then how can it now be so lush and healthy here?"

"Well, I was here when it all began. Somehow man succeeded in planting trees, and then something incredible happened: more plants, flowers and even trees, which were not planted by man, somehow seemed to grow out of nowhere!"

"Are you saying the bacteria that made me sick and caused my indigestion are now gone from here?"

"No," said the squirrel. "The bacteria that cause stomach aches and intestinal pains are still there, but thanks to reforestation, there are millions of other bacteria, good bacteria, in the soil. Now they have outnumbered the bacteria which made you sick!"

"So are you sure I am not going to have diarrhea again the moment I drink here?"

"Absolutely not! I have been living here for five years and I've never had a problem. And that's also thanks to all the mushrooms that grow around the roots of these trees and plants."

The deer looked surprised. "You must be making a mistake. Mushrooms do not grow on roots, they grow on wood, or straw or even coffee-waste."

"That is true, but there are mushrooms which act like the saliva in your mouth. They digest food for the tree and then the tree can absorb it better and grow faster - and that's exactly how it all began!"

"How fascinating, trees also have saliva! But I hope they do not spit like lamas and people do! "

© 2001 Pauli

An Inspiration for Management:
DIVERSIFICATION

Creativity and innovation can strengthen the present product portfolio, identifying new products which are part of the present production system. If products are identified in this way, they will automatically increase cash flow, simultaneously reducing risks. **Innovation emanating from core products implies fewer risks.**

Creative thinking leads to results we could not have anticipated. Therefore, by searching for increased levels of productivity, better margins and more attractive ways to respond to consumer needs, it is best to first assess what you already have. In other words, the best way to leap forward is by building on what you already have, instead of jumping into completely new fields. **Base diversity on what you have.**

The building up of a portfolio of products and services which create a cluster around the original core business leads to the creation of a lotus flower effect: many petals will open up the first day, but will not continue to open every day thereafter. **Diversify into a cluster and keep in mind a keen sense of timing.**

TOMATOES AND SKIN CARE AT UNILEVER

Originally, when Lever Brothers established its business worldwide for home and personal care products based on vegetable oil (mainly palm and coconut), it had to deal with a lot of waste that was actually a useful ingredient for the food business. When the Dutch arm of the Unilever group entered the vegetable oils business from a food perspective, it realized that many of its left-over products represented ideal inputs for home and personal care. It was a logical development that these two corporations merged to create Unilever some 75 years ago. The British headquarters remain very focused on home and personal care, and the Dutch headquarters remain very focused on the food business. It is a unique company with two chairmen and two headquarters but a clear coherence of operations which was never forced to demerge and focus on each core business.

Whereas the logic was obvious with the processing of vegetable oil, some of that original drive towards efficiencies has been lost over the years. The portfolio of some 400 brands which include Bertolli, Lipton, Dove and Ben & Jerry ice-cream requires a delicate planning of the supply chain management. Unilever is one of the largest processors of tomatoes, only matched by Heinz Ketchup which has a clear core business approach. With an estimated 1.65 million tons of fruits (tomato is not a vegetable) converted into tomato sauce annually, Unilever is one of the leading companies in the world market. Like any process, the conversion of a tomato into a sauce generates some waste. It is quite minimal but still amounts to some 30,000 tons annually.

The main composition of the waste is the skin and the seeds. Originally, all waste is simply dumped or shipped off to local farmers whereby Unilever would carry the shipment cost. Inspired by a "closed loop" production system, the tomato skin is ground into fine pieces and reintroduced into the tomato sauce. The seeds, however, are too acidic and would alter the taste of the sauce and therefore remain outside of the production system.

Though the skin is rich in lycopenes, a biochemical known as a carotenoid, which is better than betacarotene, made carrots popular as a healthy food. The question that should be raised is why does one wish to push the lycopenes into the tomato sauce at an internal transfer price of US$400 per ton, when the personal care division cannot afford these biochemicals since at US$8,000 a ton these are considered too expensive. The skin also includes some natural color pigments, which are needed in the ice-cream business. The same applies to the seeds which are rich in poly-unsaturated and mono-unsaturated fatty acids, another welcome ingredient in the personal care and cosmetics industry.

If a company depends for a major part of its ingredients on agriculture, it is a great opportunity to diversify into additional products of higher value that would simply not fetch the price if it were merely reintroduced into the core business, diversification makes sense.

Diversify within the existing production system - And not in the market segment
Diversify based on what you already have
Build a cluster with a sense of timing

Let us plant trees to enhance the ecology of the forest!

"Product Design"

Walking on Water

The frog is sad, because his two baby frogs are very ill. Swimming through the water, he is looking for help and clues on what has caused this family's illness. But no one can help. The fish, the algae, the crustaceans and plankton, everyone is ill, but no one knows why.

Then he notices a family of water striders, who normally walk on water, but now are standing on the shore.

"Do you know why everyone is feeling so sick?" the frog calls over to the water insects.

"It seems there are a lot of heavy metals in the water," replies the insect with the longest legs.

"Heavy metals have been around for years, and it never affected us before," responds the frog. "We amphibians have a natural protection against it."

"Well insects are not affected by the heavy metals either, but we have another problem... we cannot walk on the water anymore."

"I noticed. You normally walk criss-cross over the water and now you are standing on the shore – why?"

"Because there are too many detergents!"

"Detergents, I thought they are used to clean clothes, removing the dirt from the textiles before it goes back into the water."

"No, detergents and soaps make water wetter!" replies one of the insects.

"What use is wetter water?" sighs the frog, who wants to go on looking for help for his babies.

"You see if water is wetter, then it washes better... because the water tension is lower, so it can penetrate the fiber in clothes easier. And when this happens, then the tension in the water is not enough for us to walk on it!"

"That is terrible, what will you do?" croaks the frog.

"We have been waiting for months for the water to be less wet, but there are now so many detergents we will have to move away from here."

"But if these detergents change the water tension, then the heavy metals which were always in the water will now penetrate my skin..." whispers the frog.

"That is why 'washing white' is toxic!" cries out the insect.

© 2001 Pauli

An Inspiration for Management:
PRODUCT DESIGN

The design of a product requires more than just responding to the obvious needs of potential clients. Being innovative and creative is all very well, but it also requires insight and understanding that whenever there are changes and novelties, there are also uncertainties. **Innovation creates uncertainties beyond what can be foreseen.**

Uncertainties must be mitigated by building up the necessary experience, because not everything can be foreseen. Therefore, one must clearly assess the potential liabilities of various products. How can one deal with the famous "Factor X" which no one could have imagined, yet it still occurs? **A desire to innovate requires a commitment to accept responsibility for the outcome.**

When we design a new product or a manufacturing system, then we must consider not only the impact on the market, and our profits, but also the impact on nature and future generations. Consider how this innovation will impact the next seven generations from today? **Innovation considers not only the risks for today, but the risks of tomorrow and for decades to come.**

SÖDRA CELL AND ZERO TOLERANCE ON CHLORINE

The making of paper is an established technology. The felled trees are transported to a pulping mill where chemicals separate the three core components of wood: the cellulose which provides the structural strength of the wood, the lignin which is like the glue that holds the cellulose together and the hemicellulose which is like the food for the tree. Paper is made of cellulose and some fillers. The hemicellulose is quickly washed away, but the lignin has to be chemically removed. That is why there is a need for alkali sulfates.

The problem is that if one wishes to burn all the lignin away, more and harsher chemicals need to be used. If not all lignin is removed, paper will turn yellow when exposed to the sun. That is why newspapers change color so rapidly in the presence of sun rays; this cheaper variety of paper has a good tensile strength needed to print thousands of copies quickly, but still includes about 10% lignin. The nice office paper has not only been delignified it has also been treated chemically with chlorine to not only create but also maintain the white color effect.

This was the standard of the industry. Everyone around the world applied the same technique. Slowly but steadily the use of chlorine started raising some questions, especially when it became apparent that this lead to the creation of dioxin, a highly toxic man-made chemical that accumulated in the river and lake beds around the pulping mills. Several environmental organizations started campaigning against the use of chlorine and it even resulted in boycott which was quite successful in Germany. When consumers in the largest market in Europe start to express their misgivings about chlorinated paper, someone has to react.

The main supplier of pulp and paper reacted by arguing that chlorine was under control, the pollution was minimal, eventually only measurable in one per hundreds of millions, even only one in a billion. But the consumer organizations were not satisfied. If dioxin is known to cause cancer, how can you discharge only a little bit? You cannot be acknowledging that you only cause a little bit of cancer. It was in the wake of this debate that a small Swedish pulp producer, Södra Cell, decided to commit to zero chlorine. This cooperative of foresters clearly saw the writing on the wall. Chlorine and dioxin were diagnosed and recognized as problem chemicals. Instead of losing the debate on less chemicals, they opted for alternative bleaching techniques (ozone and hydrogen peroxide) which lead to the same results and quickly gained the sympathy of the German market where they were able to solidify their market position. By the year 2000, all pulp and paper producers in Europe had been forced to change their mind, and chlorine has been eliminated across the board.

Innovation creates uncertainties
Translating creativity into products implies accepting responsibility for good and bad
Creativity and innovation implies risks for seven generations

Let us design detergents that do not make the frogs sick!

"Product Certification"

Bison love Spinach

A herd of bison arrives at the Picuris Pueblo in New Mexico. A young bull is very happy to get back to his roots.

"It is so nice to finally be back home," says the adolescent bull.

"Absolutely," replies the grandma bison, who is proud of her grandchild, "I love to show our ancient rock gardens."

"Rock gardens? Who likes to see rocks, which you cannot eat anyway? I want tasty bison grasses, wonderful native corn and even wild spinach!" says the grandchild.

"Spinach we have plenty of. But you are too young to know how important rock gardens are in our history," replies grandma bison.

"The one thing I do know is when I bite a rock I could break a tooth."

"You have been away from your homeland for too long. Rocks are not for animals to chew on. Rocks are great for plants to grow on. Look at these beautiful spiral gardens where you can grow blue, red and yellow corn."

"Now you are teasing me. I only know gold-colored corn."

"No, no, no, the corn has all colors of the rainbow; we even have yellow corn with a dark blue cover, which is a great fungus."

"And you want me to eat this corn? It looks bad."

"Well, your forefathers and my mother used to eat this every fall so we would be ready for winter. "

"How can this-funny looking corn ever be good for you?"

"Well as long as you do not know how rocks grow veggies, and blue mould makes you strong, you better stay with me and learn from the great tradition of our agriculture."

"Agriculture? Grandma, I want agro-business. I want more food for all of us in the herd, and want to earn more money."

"How will you do this?" wonders grandma.

"I learned that we can grow everything naturally. If we get a seal of approval from the white man who calls this organic, which means there are no chemicals in our meat, then they will pay much more." explains the bull proudly.

"I do not care what is not in there. I want to know what we get in. I want to fill our food with the best of our land. I want our culture back. I want to have agriculture!" snaps grandma quickly.

"Grandma, the white man will pay more for certified organic food."

"The white man will pay even much more if it has been Certified by our Elders, who want us to discover the wisdom of our land, and produce the best. And they want you to be you! No one else but the bison can offer it all."

© 2001 Pauli

An Inspiration for Management:
CERTIFICATION

Companies who go beyond what is required by law in terms of health, safety and quality actually welcome certification of their performance by third parties. Whereas "certified organic" was unheard of as a mainstream label for industry, it is in growing demand by consumers, especially after the dioxin and BSE (mad cow disease) scare. **Certification demonstrates excellence,** which is easily recognized by third parties. Therefore, this is an interesting tool to use in order to communicate leadership to the consumer.

But certificates are a response to specific issues. Organic farming emerged at a time when there was excessive use of pesticides like DDT. There is a need to go beyond existing certificates and ensure that these are not hampering creativity in the future. 'Once organic ... always organic,' once ISO 14,000 always 14,000. What is new? Where is the encouragement for further development and improvement? **Certification cannot become an obstacle to innovation.**

Companies have to differentiate themselves by identifying new standards on the market, which responds to new needs and interests from the consumer. These certificates should spell out **what is 'in' the product, what is innovative about the product and not just what is not in the product.**

A VISION FOR TIERRA WOOLS

Forest fires have traumatized the South West of the United States. Every summer thousands of hectares of prime forest land goes up in smoke. The proposal is to eliminate the small-diameter wood, which can never grow to maturity. The thin trees, which are the cause of rapidly spreading fires, are cut with a chainsaw greased with a vegetable oil that is inoculated with local mushroom species, an invention patented by the mushroom expert Paul Stamets. So instead of cutting the forest, one is seeding mushrooms! The twigs and leaves or needles are converted to animal feed using other fungi, offering feed for sheep which are accused of causing soil erosion.

When Hernán Cortez arrived in Mexico, the Aztecs were devastated with the arrival of the horses. But Cortez also brought with him sheep, which became a tradition amongst the early Hispanic communities which settled in the US South West. The *churro* and the *rambouillet* sheep represent 450 years of tradition and culture. These sheep not only represent the traditions of the Hispanic settlers, these animals were embraced by the Native Americans, especially the Hopi and the Navajo nations which found a unique chance to use their exceptional skills in applying natural colors extracted from local plants and insects.

Since environmentalists criticized the sheep farmers for ruining the land, even to the point that they would file a lawsuit prohibiting the state and federal government from leasing grazing land to the sheep herders in an effort to stop soil erosion. In the meantime, synthetic colors have overtaken natural colors so that the tradition of the Indian nations is at risk of being lost. The cooperative of women, Tierra Wools, with two decades of experience in the poorest communities in Northern New Mexico, introduced a sweater made from wool from organically farmed sheep, and colored with the natural pigments of the region.

This sweater is beautiful and is more than just a sweater. This could become a symbol of the fight against soil erosion, the fight against forest fires. It reintroduces the biodiversity of mushrooms and stimulates demand for natural color pigments which do not need any irrigation. This is representative of the tradition of the Hispanic community and a showcase for the culture of the Navajo and Hopi nations. This sweater is more than organic; not only are there no chemicals and toxins used, it is also rich in culture and tradition and as a result can be sold at a premium price as soon as one gets the marketing right.

Certification confirms excellence
Certification cannot be an obstacle to innovation
Certify what is in the product, and not what is not in the product

Let us get into agriculture certified by the Elders!

"Ethics in Business"

Why can't I steal less?

John goes to church and confesses to the priest that he has been stealing.

"But," he promises, "from now on, I will steal less. Will I be a good boy?"

"No my son," responds the priest, "that is not enough. You cannot simply steal less... you cannot steal anything at all!"

John looks down and suggests: "I have been stealing so much, I cannot stop at once. I should be able to steal a little in the meantime."

"No," insists the priest calmly, "you cannot steal less... a thief is a thief."

John tries again: "But I promise you, I will only steal during the weekends, not during the week. Am I not a good boy during the week?"

"No!," says the priest raising his voice, "if you have been stealing for so long from your community, the time has come to do something in return and show that you are sorry for what you have done."

"In a few years, I promise, when I am not stealing anymore, I will do something for all of you."

"Stop it will you? If you continue thinking and acting that way you will end up in hell."

After a moment of silence, the boy murmurs: "But then my dad will end up in hell as well."

"What? Your dad? He is not a thief, I know him very well."

"No, no you are right. My father is not a thief," rebukes the boy quickly.

"So why do you say that? He has a factory, makes good products, offers well-paying jobs, built the local hospital, organizes cultural programs, and last year he even got the environment prize from the community for reducing toxic waste by 80%. Your father is a hero. He will never go to hell."

The boy remains silent for a moment, then looks the priest in the eye and asks him: "How come I will go to hell for stealing less, and my dad is a hero for polluting less. He is still polluting with toxic waste."

© 2001 **Pauli**

An Inspiration for Management:
ETHICS IN BUSINESS

Companies have to succeed in making a product of good quality, offered at a competitive price, and available on time. This is a minimum requirement and what everyone strives for. But in reality products must have more depth and call for an emotional bond. This requires an unequivocal product design, a transparent manufacturing system and a

respect for basic principles such as no child labor and no toxic products. This is known as CSR, corporate social responsibility. **Product innovation goes beyond just the product and the manufacturing process.**

New business opportunities were once based on the SWOTS analysis (strengths, weaknesses, opportunities and threats) as taught in business school. Today, if a company has a small but highly sensitive weakness, it can jeopardize the overall business. Therefore, management must keep an eye on all operations and make certain that there are no hiccups in any of the basic ethics of its business. **Your successes may be based on your main competitors' weaknesses.**

The ethical standards against which companies are judged evolve over time. Future generations will be much harsher. Wasting waste will not be tolerated, just like stealing *just a little* cannot be tolerated. Companies will have to become innovative in ethics, sensing the demands for higher moral standards by future generations, thanks to the information age. **Innovation in ethics and CSR is now key for corporations.**

DuPont Goes for Zero Accidents, Zero Waste and Zero Emissions

DuPont is one of the oldest chemical groups in the world. It is the inventor of household names such as nylon, without which stockings would simply not have been able to be mass produced, and Teflon, which makes it possible to cook without the food sticking to the frying pan. DuPont was the largest producer of CFC, the chemicals which powered spray cans, but which adversely affected the ozone layer, leading to rapid destruction of this protective layer blocking out UV rays, which dramatically increased the risk of skin cancer. DuPont at first objected to the regulation and the banning of CFCs, but then decided to side with the environmentalists and banned this substance.

Under the leadership of their chairman, Edgar Woolard, DuPont went a step further than merely banning harmful chemicals, it committed to "The Goal is Zero" strategy: zero accidents, zero waste and zero emissions. In 1993, the chairman had his 80 top managers sign the commitment and had it published internationally. How could one tolerate an accident? A company with over 100,000 employees cannot claim that a 0.01% risk does materialize. After all, this would imply accepting that each year 10 employees would suffer a fatal accident on the premises. The goal can only be zero accidents. This does not mean that no accidents happen, but the commitment has to be one without any compromise.

The same logic applies to toxic waste substances. If a company is aware of the fact that it is discharging large amounts of toxins, then the first step may indeed be to document and control these so as to ensure that the business remains within the limits permitted by law, or prescribed by the license to operate. But once the company realizes that the discharge of noxious materials into the air, water or soil includes elements which are harmful to people and the environment, then there is only one target acceptable: zero!

Paul Tebo, the health, safety and environment manager of DuPont, had a clear task: eliminate the toxins and go after each substance that should not be released. Even better, search for uses within the group so that whatever was a toxin for one facility, could actually be re-used as an input for another industrial process. And if, after due consideration, management comes to the conclusion that this particular product or process will never be able to meet the standard of zero, which is one without any form of compromise, then DuPont has the option to disinvest. It positioned DuPont solidly against its main competitors who are not able to take such a bold step, and as such are vulnerable in the eyes of the policy-makers and the environmental organizations. Competition moves from building on your strengths to eliminating your weaknesses.

Product innovation must go beyond the product
Innovation is measured against the weakness of your
main competitors
Pioneer the cutting edge through ethical behavior -
the gift is innovation

Let us stop stealing altogether!

"Creativity"

The Zebra Aircon

Termites are building a hill next to a herd of zebras.

"How nice that we have our chimney nearly ready," says the master builder termite.

"Chimney? Are you making a fire in your home?" wonders the zebra.

"No, we only need to let the hot air go out, so that the cool air can come in."

"I thought a chimney was needed to let the hot air out when you make a fire because it is cold outside?"

"No, termites make chimneys to let hot air *out* when it is warm!"

"I see, hot air goes up and as the hot air leaves through a chimney, fresh air is pulled in through underground pipes."

"Exactly. All buildings, especially skyscrapers, should all have chimneys on their roofs," confirms the termite.

"Skyscrapers should not only have big chimneys to let the hot air out and the cold air in, they should paint the building black and white, like a zebra!"

"You must be mistaken. Buildings should be painted white, since white reflects the sun, which would keep the inside cool," responds the termite.

"No, no, no learn from the zebra, just look around you!"

"The zebra is black and white, but the black stripes in the sun must be burning hot."

"No actually, they're not hot."

"But surely black creates heat. White makes it cool."

"That is true but the zebra has a *thick layer of fat* under the black stripes so he does not feel the heat."

"But what is the use of black making it so hot if the Zebra doesn't feel it?"

"Well, what do you think happens to the hot air?" questions the zebra.

"Mmmm. It expands, and becomes lighter... so it rises," tinkers to termite.

"Good. And what happens to the air hanging over the white stripes next to it?" insists the zebra.

"It is cooler, and expands less ... so it does not rise?" wonders the termite.

"Absolutely... and what happens when the air over the black rises?"

"Then the pressure is low," zaps back the termite.

"And what happens when the pressure goes down above the black and remains high over the white stripes?" pokes the zebra.

"Then wind flows from the white to the black ... oh now I see, it reduces the difference in pressure by creating a local wind."

"Great... now *that* is my natural air-conditioning! Do you think it would it be enough for butterflies to windsurf between the stripes?"

© **2002 Pauli**

An Inspiration for Management:
CREATIVITY

Creativity is not about finding the right answers: it is about searching for the right questions. It is not about having people around you giving you all the answers either; it is about encouraging people who make you search for more answers. **Asking questions leads to creativity.**

Questions are best directed at possible answers, which are counter-intuitive... because if the answers were assumed as logical, then there's no room left for innovation. The search is over. Therefore creativity requires an unconventional approach. **Counter-intuitivism ensures creativity.**

New insights must be practical, despite often initially appearing to be crazy. Currently no one imagines a building painted like a zebra, and yet it opens up the mind to new forms of energy, and questions the traditional way of doing things. Although the 'old way' *seems* to be working fine, it is not good enough – and data measuring the negative impacts over time should demand updating in itself. **Creativity requires vision beyond doing better the old way.**

NOVAMONT MAKES PLASTICS FROM STARCH
(EVEN BANANA PEELS)

The source for plastics is petroleum. There are hundreds of varieties of plastics made from this same macro-molecule. These products are efficient and functional, though have one problem: after use they accumulate in the environment. If one swam in the Manila Bay waters one would find thousands, if not millions, of plastic sachets, which once contained shampoo, littering the bottom of the ocean. A trip through Nigeria will convince anyone that there is a need to speed up biodegradation since these plastics just accumulate. In 2003 the government of Bangladesh banned all plastics bags since these clogged the water systems leading to massive flooding that affected one third of the population.

The making of biodegradable plastics has been attempted by numerous companies. The creation of poly-lactic acids (PLA) is one of the new standards. The chemical conversion of a natural starch into a plastic which has a predictable biodegradation is a major step forward. But biodegradation is not enough. The Cargill/Dow plastic relies on genetically modified corn, and you either eat the corn or you make a plastic from it. This creates a higher demand for corn, of course serving the business interest of Cargill. The researchers of the Kyushu Institute of Technology have a much more sustainable proposal, converting organic city waste from restaurants, supermarkets and households into the same PLA. This is biodegradable and recovers starch from waste. That means that first you eat, and from the waste you produce plastics. That is a real sustainable option. The Italian company Novamont, a research company located in Novara, Italy, brought the PLA technologies to a new level.

Starch is abundant in this world. It is present in potatoes and corn, but the richest concentrations of up to 92% are found in yucca and cassava, two staple foods in Africa and Latin America. But even banana peels are rich in starch, and one can imagine plastic bags made from banana peels or leftover cassava skin. The key to the process is to control the timing when the product can become biodegradable. Two applications have demonstrated its great value: the making of tyres and the bags protecting bananas in the field.

Goodyear realized that pollution in the cities is amongst others created by the carbon black of tyres. This core ingredient that makes up the outer casing with rubber, solely to be strengthened by a steal belt or cord, or nylon cord, is not degradable at all. That is why it represents such a problem. Novamont designed a substitute, based on starch, which will trigger degradation after ten years. This eliminates carbon black altogether and does away with a major source of air pollution. There are millions of used tyres around, ready to catch fire and causing major pollution. This risk is now designed out of the system.

Questions lead to creativity
The more counter-intuitive, the more creative
Creative vision requires going beyond solutions of the past

Let's paint our building with black and white stripes!

"Team Building"

The Strongest Tree

"How can I ever be the strongest tree in this forest?" asks the oak tree.

"The more leaves I have, the more energy I get from the sun.

And the more leaves will drop on the ground.

Ants, earthworms and mushrooms convert this into new food for me.

The more food I have, the more fruits I can grow.

The more fruit, the more birds will visit me.

The more birds, the more droppings... the more droppings, the more bacteria in the soil...

Much soil bacteria enrich the ground water.

The more food in the water, the more flowers will grow; the more flowers - the more bees...

...The more bees, the more pollination, the more seeds...

The more procreation for everyone, which is why my family and I are the strongest in the forest!

Everyone gives me many gifts, made from whatever I was not using.

And they *all* contribute to me being the strongest... some are small, some are ugly and some I can't tell the difference between their head and tail...

If I were to chase the earthworms away because I do not like or understand them, since I cannot distinguish head from tail, I could not be the strongest tree in the forest.

And if you give away (what you did not need anyway) you get a lot back, and all together we can thrive."

The tree gives away what is not needed and receives from others what they do not need.

The tree knows that everyone helps in making it the strongest in the forest, even the smallest.... and perhaps even the ugly.

© 1997 Pauli

An Inspiration for Management:
TEAM BUILDING

A business is made up of many different team members. **A diverse team means strength.** Imagine if you only had flashy salesmen or smart lawyers on the team. Or perhaps there are some members you do not like, while some you appreciate. Others you love to work with, while you have no idea why some are even there, and then there are those you never even knew were part of the team!

Where does the 'dislike' come from? Is it because of their appearance, or simply because you do not understand or cannot relate to that person and have not yet figured out what their contribution to the team is? A company can only be successful if management builds up a balanced team, where varied backgrounds, training and a broad range of characters in fact contribute to the enrichment of the company. **Strong teams mean resilience.**

Why carry the burden? A team can make the dream come true! The 'earthworm' character in the team is hardworking and does the 'dirty work' that many do not like, but someone has to do it and all tasks are equally important as they make up the whole, which is more than the sum of the parts. So if you are the leader and you wish to have the strongest and the best team, make certain that everyone contributes to the best of their capabilities. **Resilience means fast-track change.** This is entrepreneurship, creativity, innovation and leadership.

LAS GAVIOTAS (COLOMBIA)

The Environmental Research Center Las Gaviotas has about 200 employees. It is probably the most innovative technology center in the world. Its founder, Paolo Lugari, is constantly seeking to find creative solutions to the pressing problems of livelihoods. The employees are labeled as "indisciplined" persons, i.e. people who do not have one or the other specific professional background or discipline. People working in the center have to perform every job, and rotation is compulsory. The highest appreciation from the team goes to those who try the most and make errors, which are a precondition to getting better results in other, often unrelated endeavors elsewhere.

If there is one social and economic environment which requires high levels of resilience, it is Colombia. The 8,000 ha reforestation project is located in the Llanos of Vichada, on the eastern side of Colombia, close to the Orinoco River. There, the team succeeded in converting a savannah back into a rainforest. Through the plantation of a native species of pine trees, the pH of the soil shifted from 4 to 5.5 and thus made it possible for the birds, the bees and the wind to recover some 250 plant species. Even though it resembled monoculture, given that it was a local species, it soon became a breeding ground for biodiversity. The ground water, which originally was a main cause of gastro-intestinal diseases, is now of drinking quality, and has become a major source of preventive medicine.

The monitoring of the newly-created forest is secured by airships, equipped with infrared that spot a local rise in temperature early on so that it can be extinguished within 15 minutes. The forest provides numerous products, including a resin tapped from the trees which is processed locally into colofonia, an additive to the paper and paint industry. The forest also provides waste wood which is used in boilers to generate energy. The whole of Las Gaviotas village is disconnected from the grid. All transportation is on bicycles, trucks are reserved for forestry work only. This has created a demand for bicycles adapted to local needs. A new factory for the assembly of electric bicycles will constitute the next industrial frontier.

On July 6, 2004 the HE Alvaro Uribe announced to decision of the Colombian Government to expand the reforestation initiative from the present 8,000 HA to 6.3 million HA. This is the largest recreation of rainforest ever attempted.

The team constructed the first hospital off the grid. It has natural air-conditioning and dehumidification systems, water purification and a solar cooking system that works on vegetable oil heated in solar systems. Las Gaviotas designed water pumps where, instead of the piston, the shaft moves, thus permitting a better pumping result with less effort. The solar water-heating system is the largest operation in Latin America with over 40,000 apartments installed with a system that has no moving parts. Therefore, Las Gaviotas can offer a 25-year warranty, something which is unheard of in the industry.

Diversity creates strength
Strength creates resilience
Resilience creates the capacity for rapid change

Let our family of trees be the strongest in the whole forest!

Epilogue
Systems Innovation

The framework of competition has changed, as it used to be a fairly transparent system where players in the market would focus on what they do best. It was the time of competition based on the strength of each of the major companies on the market. This all changed after the Americans introduced the SWOTS analysis, the famous search for strengths and weaknesses, opportunities and threats. The assessment is based on one's own strengths and weaknesses and whenever one element is considered insufficient within one company, and is recognized as a strength within another company, then an attempted 'buy out' would follow. At present we live in a competitive framework, which has further evolved. It is not the strengths or the weaknesses of oneself, but rather the weakness of the adversary on the market, which will inspire competitive strategies.

This new approach of building success through exploiting the weaknesses of competitors regardless of their experience, size or strength has many similarities to the self-defense sports aikido and judo. Whatever the size of the opponent, the weakness of the opponents will be used to beat them. Even the powerful adversary's muscular strength can be used to his disadvantage. It is an ingenuous system, one that offers young and inexperienced entrepreneurs the chance to imagine an entry into the market even in the wake of mighty market players. It implies that the market players themselves cannot rest on their credentials of the past, nor on their powerful position today and will have to scrutinize themselves continuously to secure the never-ending elimination of numerous weaknesses, which may have remained unnoticed. The era of total quality management has been confirmed.

It is against this background that companies need to reassess their innovation strategies. It is not possible to maintain present market share and internal rate of returns unless companies embark on an aggressive program to stimulate creativity as a basis for business development, reaching ever more competitive levels, as weaknesses continue to be addressed.

Three Types of Innovation

Business has traditionally focused on two types of innovation: product and process. The time has come to introduce a third type: *systems* innovation... The difference is fundamental, the impact is pervasive. *And,* the opportunities that emerge from this third way of designing innovations are the one that will make a solid breakthrough in corporate strategies to channel creativity.

The difference between product and system innovation is perhaps best demonstrated by the drive of corporations to improve quality. At first, when companies defined the quality of a product, manufacturing would then match the product manufactured with the agreed standard. Later this evolved into a process technology. When a company is certified ISO 9,000, then it has not agreed on detailed product quality specifications. On the contrary, the company will ensure through a total quality management program, that whatever is being produced will be of great quality and will always be up for further improvements. Business needs to be more flexible and able to adjust to ever-changing needs on the market with numerous models. A company like General Motors could theoretically sell one billion varieties of cars and trucks using all possible combinations of models and options. It is impossible to define a quality specification for each model sold to the client. It is the *process* that leads to quality standards, which are self-imposed.

The same goes for innovation. Instead of searching for a new product, or improvement of a process, the company will have to reorganize business in an effort to secure that there will always be innovations both in products, processes as well as continuously improving the entire system. There is no need to focus on specific targets; the management system will be conducive to a creative atmosphere that leads to a never-ending flow of innovations which will permeate business activities at all levels.

The shift from a product, to a process to a *systems* innovation is demonstrated in the hypothetical case of sugar. This natural sweetener is originally derived from sugarcane. This has lead to the massive cultivation of cane throughout the tropics, from Cuba and Brazil, Fiji and Okinawa (Japan), South Africa and Zimbabwe. Sugar from sugar cane has not been so popular lately since it is recognized that it creates cavities in teeth and leads to weight gain. Therefore, sugar has been substituted by a new product - saccharine or aspartame. The product sugar-from-cane is substituted by saccharine and aspartame. This is a product innovation.

As consumers are prepared to pay 50 times the price of sugar for this new sweetener, the world market price for sugarcane tumbled. The sugarcane processing industry is perhaps focusing on the incorrect component. Indeed, the sweetener from sugarcane also brings with it the risk of diabetes. The major part of the sugarcane is actually never consumed… the bulk of what's left after processing out sugar is bagasse – and this is incinerated in an effort to recover some energy which contributes to carbon dioxide emissions.

Yet sugarcane could be used for the very efficient production of pulp fibers for paper. The problem is that the traditional alkali sulfate processing technique for making paper from the cellulose of a tree does not offer good results with bagasse. The reason is easy to understand. The processing of a tree must be different from the processing of a grass (sugarcane is a grass). Thus, here is a need for a process innovation. This process innovation is difficult for the leading paper and pulp companies to implement. After all, there is no sugarcane in Scandinavia or Canada. Innovation can therefore be expected from new players who can exploit the weakness of the largest producers of pulp in the world. The introduction of the innovative processes like steam explosion, which leads to the perfect separation of cellulose, hemicelluloses, lipids and lignin, represents a major breakthrough. Processing pulp from trees with processing pulp from sugarcane represents a process innovation.

Indeed, if the traditional paper makers plant trees (even genetically manipulated and non-native in the regions where planted), these can generate no more than 20% fiber on an average of seven years after planting. That is a fraction of the fibers generated by sugarcane - which grows to maturity in less than eight months producing a left-over with up to 80% in fiber! Therefore, one can expect up to 30 times more fiber from sugarcane than from trees *per hectare per year*. That is hard to beat and, if successful, this process could jeopardize the long-term investments of forestry. These traditional market-players who invested in tree-farming will naturally resist this innovative process. Research in the forestry industry will now search for extremely low marginal cost prices to defend their market position, locking in supply and clients through long-term delivery contracts. Since the investment in a new pulping plant reaches US$ 500 million, as much as a modern microprocessor factory, it is understandable that the market leaders will do whatever is needed to avoid any innovation outside their core business to take place.

The next step is a systems innovation. Imagine if the sugarcane is used to make sugar, at very low cost. The sugar is not farmed to sweeten our meals but is used instead to make biodegradable *plastics*, substituting many petroleum-based plastics. The residual bagasse is treated to remove all lignin (*delignified*) and is used to generate fiber. The fibers are then processed using new technologies. The lignin, which has a high calorific value, is now used as an energy source. Sugarcane is now the basis for three commercial products: *plastics, fiber* and *energy*. This is a system innovation of the first type. Whereas the making of plastics from sugar would be uncompetitive compared to petrochemical plastics, if one can cross-finance the three products, then these also become competitive as a cluster. As individual entities, these businesses stand no chance; together they beat the standard on the market.

This type of systems creativity will offer innovative companies a major edge over those who are only seeking to improve an existing product or tooling around an existing process. *System innovation with improvements in productivity* increases jobs as well as having a positive impact on the people and the ecosystem. And the people, who design, implement and operate these systems in co-evolution with nature, have a joy so powerful that it will be felt by their children seven generations down the line.

"There is nothing more difficult to take in hand,
more perilous to conduct,
or more uncertain in its success, than to take the lead
in introduction of a new order of things,
because the innovator has for enemies
all those who have done well under the old conditions,
and lukewarm defenders
in those who may do well under the new."

Machiavelli in The Prince

Out of the Box - ZERI-Rap by Simon Vasquez

"Out Da Box"
text by Simon VASQUEZ © 2002 Vasquez

una mano lava la otra y las dos lavan la cara

We were born to the Earth and yet we hang her
It's time to help the Five Kingdoms of Nature
And Clean up our acts and stick to the facts
When you move to the future you can't go back
Learn the new ways and don't stay in the daze
The ZERI curriculum is all the craze
Too much waste and what to do not a clue
ZERI can teach you a thing or two
One kingdom's waste is another's treasure
To the bird it's waste but to the tree it's pure pleasure
The benefit there is beyond one's measure
So wake up and snap
We are making electricity from ordinary crap
I know it sounds funny but it's true
What do you think about that
ZERI is a way that's flowing real hot
It's time to start thinking out da box

What the future has hidden ZERI unlocks
It's time to start thinking out da box
Wisdom from the past once lost
Now it's rediscovered at ZERI's cost
It is time to start thinking out da box

We are the only species that creates hazardous waste
No other species destroys the Earth's face

But the grass is green the sky is blue

You think it is a simple treat
but there is more to understand between the two
like how they work together and how we help
we need to work together it is not about self
helping the environment will help your health
unlocking the secrets of mother nature's wealth
I don't think it makes sense to waste water in flush
We need to use something that won't cost as much
It is the purest substance now we turn it toxic
We're the human race against natural logic
And that's crazy, it's just crazy

What the future has hidden ZERI unlocks
It is time to start thinking out da box
Wisdom from the past once lost
Now it's discovered at ZERI's cost
It's time to start thinking out da box

Soluciones limitadas ZERI nos saca
Es tiempo de pensar fuera de la caja
Soluciones limitadas ZERI nos saca
Es tiempo de pensar fuera de la caja

En los tiempos antes de nuestra cultura
La gente no hacia tanta basura
Tenemos que limpiar nuestro pais
Tenemos que guardar la semilla de mais
Limpiar la tierra con enzimas de lombriz
Y en esta realidad andaremos feliz
Andaremos feliz. Andaremos feliz.

La madurez consiste en realisar los suenos
Nunca dejemos de so-ar
Nunca dejemos de so-ar
Nunca dejemos de so-ar.

ABOUT THE AUTHOR

Gunter Pauli is an entrepreneur, creative and innovative in business, culture, environment and science. His palmares shows both successes and failures. He has published 12 books translated in 12 languages. He graduated from a Jesuit University, obtained his MBA and has always worked for himself. Fluent in 7 languages, having lived in Japan, USA, Sweden, having visited over 100 countries, he is a world citizen. He is impatient, and always ready to risk his name and money in innovative ventures.

His preferred scenario is the one of David versus Goliath... knowing that David will win. He has established several companies, has given briefs to heads of state on economics and geopolitics, has worked extensively with the United Nations and Development Bank and is a popular speaker to management. He is the author of children's books and designs educational systems from kindergarten to post-graduate.

BOOKS PUBLISHED BY THE SAME AUTHOR

Pauli, Gunter. "The Crusader for the Future. Portrait of Aurelio Peccei", founder of the Club of Rome. 1987, Pergamon Press, Oxford, UK. Published in English only.

Pauli, Gunter. "Services: the driving force of the economy". 1987, Waterlow Press, London, UK. Translated into Dutch, French, Norwegian.

Wright, Richard and Gunter Pauli, "The Second Wave: Japan's Global Assault on Finance". 1987, Waterlow Press, London, UK and St. Martin's Press, New York, USA. Translated into French, Japanese, Italian.

Pauli, Gunter. "Thinking and Doing: an Autobiography". 1989, Roularta Books, Brussels, Belgium. Published in Dutch only.

Pauli, Gunter. "Double Digit Growth: how to do it!". 1991, Pauli Publishing, Keerbergen, Belgium. Published in English, German, Dutch, French, Swedish.

Pauli, Gunter. "Andorra: Strategies for the Future". 1992, Published by Credit Andorra, Andorra and London, UK. Published in Catalan, English and Spanish.

Capra, Fritjof and Gunter Pauli (eds). "Steering business towards sustainability". 1995, United Nations University Press, Tokyo, Japan. Published in English and Japanese.

Pauli, Gunter. "Breakthroughs: what business can do for society". 1996, Epsilon Press, UK. Published in Italian, Spanish, Korean, Portuguese.

Pauli, Gunter. "UpSizing: More Income, More Jobs and No Waste", 1997, Greenleaf UK. Published in Italian, Spanish, Japanese, German, Portuguese, Chinese.

Pauli, Gunter. "Diversification in the Tropics". 1999, SENA, Bogota, Colombia. Published in Spanish only.

Pauli, Gunter. "Give a lot - Get a lot: a book about virtues inspired by Nature". 1999, Universidad de Manizales, Caldas, Colombia. Published in Spanish only.

Pauli Gunter. "The Strongest Tree in the Whole Forest". 2000, The World Expo, Hannover, Germany. Published in 27 languages (and subsequently 36 fairy tales).

Pauli, Gunter. "From Fairy Tales to Reality". 2003, City of Curitiba, Brazil. Published in Portuguese and Spanish.

Pauli, Gunter. "36 Fairy Tales: To Never Stop Dreaming". 2004, co-edition with Hogares Juveniles Campecinos, Bogota, Colombia. Published in Spanish, Portuguese and English.

www.zeri.org
for information on ZERI Management Training Programs write to info@zeri.org